Movement
Your Child's First Language

How movement and music
assists brain development
in children aged 3–7 years

Sally Goddard Blythe

Music and Songs by
Michael Lazarev

Hawthorn Press

Movement: Your Child's First Language © 2018 Sally Goddard Blythe and Michael Lazarev.

Sally Goddard Blythe and Michael Lazarev are hereby identified as the authors of this work in accordance with section 77 of the Copyright, Designs and Patent Act, 1988. They assert and give notice of their moral right under this Act.

Published by Hawthorn Press, Hawthorn House,
1 Lansdown Lane, Stroud, Gloucestershire, GL5 1BJ, UK
Tel: (01453) 757040
E-mail: info@hawthornpress.com
Website: www.hawthornpress.com

Cover illustration © Getty Images
Cover design by Bruce Winslade
Illustrations by Sharon Rentta and Tom Kerr
Typesetting by Winslade Graphics, Stroud, Gloucestershire, GL5 2AJ
Printed by Short Run Press Ltd, Exeter 2018, 2019.

Every effort has been made to trace the ownership of all copyrighted material. If any omission has been made, please bring this to the publisher's attention so that proper acknowledgement may be given in future editions.

Printed on paper sourced from sustained managed forests and elemental chlorine free.

British Library Cataloguing in Publication Data applied for.

ISBN 978-1-907359-99-6

For children
of the future

'I returned, and saw under the sun, that the race is not to the swift, nor the battle to the strong, neither yet bread to the wise, nor yet riches to men of understanding, nor yet favour to men of skill; but time and chance happens to them all.'

Ecclesiastes 9:11

Taking Time

When I slow down
I can smell autumn in the air;
Hear the rustle of fallen leaves underfoot
And feel the dampness in my hair.

When I slow down
I feel like a child again;
Excited, curious, strangely alone
in this magical world
which, in this moment
is all mine.

I could be the only person on the planet
in this vast space,
this world of colour,
floating, free.

In a minute, in an hour, tomorrow
it will all be gone
never to be the same again;
like the sun setting in the evening sky,
light on the water reflecting rustic hues as they are now.

In this moment, this now,
I and the world are at one.
I am and I am complete.

Killing Time

I cannot hear the words of my lover
As he calls to speak to me.
His words drowned by the sounds of traffic,
of sirens and people, people everywhere.

A colony of human ants,
swerving at the last moment to avoid contact.
Neither touching, nor speaking
Not looking anyone in the eye.

Ears plugged, phone in hand,
talking into an invisible space
occluding the world outside.
No time to see what lies between,
cocooned in a bespoke world of their own.

Time and space their enemy,
to be controlled, overcome or contained.
Time accelerated the faster they go.
Digital people who have become the unwitting slaves of time.

Life lived in the fast lane,
exciting, cool, important and so, so busy.
Keeping up, staying ahead
Speculating on what is coming next.

And yet, the folly of time is
that the news of today will be of no use tomorrow.
It matters only now.

Contents

Acknowledgements

Michael Lazarev for permission to publish his songs and music.

Sharon Rentta for illustrations included in the stories *Early Morning by the Pond*, *A Day in the Garden* and *Wings of Childhood*.

Parents and children for permission to use photographs of them.

Martin Large for commissioning this book.

All at Hawthorn Press for their support, attention to detail and taking this book from an idea to publication.

Chapter 1

Are You Sitting Comfortably?

First Language

'Are you sitting comfortably? Then I'll begin.' Those are the words I heard every week day in the first years of my life before I started school.

I was one of a whole generation of children who grew up listening to *Listen with Mother* (1950–1982). Few families had televisions in those days, and for those who did, daytime television did not exist. *Listen with Mother* comprised a story and nursery rhymes, and more than 50 years later I can still remember the names and voices of the presenters, the words to the nursery rhymes and some of the stories, even though I was under four years of age and had not learned to read. Why should these early memories have remained and still be so clear more than half a century later?

Today, it is visual technology which dominates our lives, and while visual information, like the speed of light, is processed faster than sound, listening involves a different form of attention. Listening involves translating streams of sounds into visual images to create pictures in the mind (meaning) and working memory to remember sequences of information.

The written word evolved from an oral tradition in which knowledge, wisdom and folk lore were passed down from one generation to the next through the spoken word – the telling of stories and singing of songs. Children of today are no different from our ancestors in the sense that every child is born from the same pre-natal environment as its forebears, but each generation enters an increasingly complex world in which an ever-increasing range of skills must be learned from scratch.

Children naturally tend to replicate their evolutionary development through play, starting with simple physical activities such as chasing, play fighting and building before progressing to the more recent 'cognitive' skills increasingly required in modern technological societies. In these same societies, there is an impatience to reach the end goal without traversing all the stepping stones along the way. Such accelerationism in learning runs the risk of developing higher skills without first putting firm foundations in place.

Can *you* remember how it felt to curl up at night for a bedtime story, turning the pages, pretending to 'read' from the pictures while listening to your parent telling the tale? How words gradually started to form as pictures in your mind and to make sense from the patterns of letters on the page? Can you still remember the magical thinking of childhood, when you could see pictures in the clouds and believe that anything was possible? This is the language of childhood.

The inner world of childhood is very different from the thinking world we inhabit as adults. It is a world dominated by sensation and constant discovery; of learning how to control the body and to 'make sense' of experience derived from the different senses; of translating sensation into perception, and perception into thought and action.

Learning to crawl, walk, talk, listen and read strongly influence the opportunities a child will later have to improve their own well-being and life chances. Whilst some of these skills are innate, others must be passed from one generation to the next, and this happens through providing a child with opportunity, time and experiences that carefully build their understanding and the neural pathways that support it.

In the first few years of life, a child's brain develops rapidly, driven by a mix of experience, environment and genes. It is known from the field of neuroscience that periods of rapid neural development are accompanied by accelerated learning, and the pre-school years are unique in this respect. Conversely, these same periods are particularly vulnerable to injury, abuse or neglect, and as children grow older it becomes more difficult to influence how the brain processes information.

Of the 100 billion cells that are present at birth, only a fraction of this number will actually be used during the span of its life. Between 15 months and six years of age, the cerebral cortex (the seat of cognition) appears to double in size with synaptic density reaching its peak at about three to three and a half years of age, a level 50% higher than it was at birth, or will be at puberty.

In the beginning, neurons are unspecialised – not 'primed' for any particular function. This is known as 'equal potential', meaning flexibility of function. During the course of development, constant interaction with the environment or experience stimulates the formation of connections within the brain, particularly connections to higher or 'executive' centres that will eventually command the whole. The first years of life are the time for forming and organising these connections.

As neurons migrate, so they become more specialised in their function. In the course of the first three years of life, the brain forms almost twice as many synapses (junctions) than it will actually use. Those that are in constant use will strengthen to form the motorways of the mind; those that are unused will either be replaced by others or will eventually disappear. During infancy, many neurons retain flexibility of function or neural 'plasticity'. In this sense, every human being is truly unique. Experiences shape the architecture of the brain but no two people ever receive *exactly* the same experience even if the genetic blueprint is identical as in the case of identical twins. Experiences may be similar, but position, timing and perspective will always be slightly different, creating a neuronal tapestry that cannot be precisely replicated in any way.

There are several stages in development when the brain goes through a period of neural housekeeping, when inactive or redundant cells are 'pruned' in a spring-cleaning exercise which sweeps away neural clutter and strengthens connections that are in regular use. One such spring-cleaning period occurs between six and a half and eight years of age, another during the teenage years, so that by the late teen years only half of the synapses that were present in the three year old remain. It is perhaps not surprising that the adolescent years are frequently described as ones of turmoil. Such vigorous pruning has both advantages and disadvantages: By removing excess pathways, interference or cross chatter is reduced, allowing for greater efficiency of functioning rather like building motorways for the mind. On the other hand, connections between neurons and their target cells in pathways that have not been used become weaker over time. This process is sometimes described as 'neuronal fitness'. Fitness of neurons is determined by success in establishing contact with other cells and passing information. Something in the process of making contact helps to protect neurons from destruction – a neurological explanation for the old adage, use it or lose it.

Developmental changes in cognition and behaviour are associated with changes in the brain and vice-versa. When looking at a child's capacity for learning we cannot separate learning from development, or development from the structure and activity of the brain. During development, the structure undergoes continuous change with nature and nurture acting as twin sculptors in this process.[1]

At the age of two, connections are being formed at twice the rate of an adult brain[2] and the first three to six years are vital years for language acquisition. The relationship between young children's brain development and the emergence of language skills is mutually reinforcing[3] whereby every new word that a child learns helps to strengthen the architecture of the brain. As that architecture is strengthened, the capacity to recognise and use new words increases, but as we shall see later, language in not an isolated skill. It is closely linked to neurological development, and development during this period is not only determined by genes, but also by the experiences and environments that support this interactive process (epigenetics). Parents and carers help to build the developing architecture of the brain through the opportunities, experiences and influences they provide, but in the pre-school years it is *preparation,* not formal instruction in reading, writing and numeracy, that children really need. Preparation involves developing the sensory-motor skills needed to support later learning and an understanding of the general before the particular.

Movement Matters

Babies are born to move. Only a few weeks after conception, cradled inside a miniature ocean of amniotic fluid, a tiny acrobat starts to perform. These movements – the first outward expression of developing life – will grow in strength, complexity and refinement over many months and years to become the physical vocabulary, which is unique to the individual.

A basic repertoire of spontaneous movements and reactions is 'hard wired' into the brain stem of all healthy children at birth, but development of movement control is an individual's story, interdependent with experience and environmental opportunity.

'Children learn with their bodies before they learn with their brains,'[4] and in this sense, movement is our first language. Long before spoken language develops we are able to understand our children's needs and moods through a combination of posture, gesture, timing and rhythm of movements and utterances. These bodily expressions of inner needs and responses to outside influences are the elements of early language, also known as non-verbal language.

Non-verbal language continues to contribute up to 90 percent to effective communication for the remainder of life. Deficit in use of non-verbal language is often a feature of autistic spectrum disorders, including Asperger's syndrome. At the lesser end of the scale, children with poorly developed non-verbal language can be at greater risk of being picked on in the playground because they lack an adequate physical vocabulary with which to read the non-verbal language of others and respond appropriately. Body language emits subliminal signals about a person's ability to handle the self, and over time, body language becomes an expression of physical literacy.

Physical literacy also supports general literacy once a child starts school. Posture, balance and coordination are all needed to support centres involved in the control of the eye movements needed for reading, hand–eye coordination involved in writing and copying, and even the ability to sit still. It has been said that the most advanced level of movement is the ability to stay totally still,[5] with stillness and poise being the end product of the ability to inhibit or suspend unnecessary movement. Mastery of movement develops through experience and practice, with the early years providing a crucial period of training.

Changes to modern life, which include the need for both parents to work, technological devices and a baby equipment industry which is adept at seducing busy parents into thinking the more they spend, the better parents they must be, have all combined to alter the nature of children's physical experience in the early years. While society changes at ever-increasing speed, the process of human development changes at a much slower evolutionary pace, and the biological and development needs of children have not altered significantly over millennia. In common with other members of our species – and humans are members of the species of mammal – the basic needs of children are warmth, nourishment, physical proximity and attachment to the primary source(s) of love, sensory experience and exploration and *engagement*. Some of the best natural playgrounds for an infant in the first weeks of life are entirely free – the mother's body – and a few weeks later, a clean blanket on the floor.

When an infant is held and its needs are met, it becomes attuned to the body language of its carer; if it is placed on a clean, safe surface when awake, it is free to wave and stretch its arms and legs, to learn where its body begins and ends in space; how to hold its head up and begin to support its own weight, eventually to roll, sit, crawl and finally stand and walk. This process of trial and error – of learning how to do something – is very different from being placed in a moulded baby seat and passively entertained by electronic media.

Canadian neuropsychologist Donald Hebb, a specialist in the field of associative learning, first described how 'neurons that fire together wire together'.[6] When areas of the body (and therefore also the brain) are exercised they mature into more specialised regions that are fine-tuned for efficient and accurate performance. Regular practice strengthens the neural pathways involved, not only refining skill but also developing specialisation of functioning, resulting in improved performance with economy of effort eventually leading to automated function. The advantages of automated function are that certain skills can be carried out without conscious awareness, only recruiting conscious effort when the situation requires it.

Examples of how movement practice at any level and stage can enhance performance can be seen in athletic training and aspects of musical performance. A study which examined differences in the practice and training techniques of professional javelin throwers found that those who practised a range of physical activities every day in addition to specific skill training showed improved performance, compared to those who had only carried out practice in javelin throwing. Similarly, the oft-loathed discipline of practising musical scales and arpeggios helps to develop finger strength, accuracy, placement (without having to look at the hands), and adaptability in reaching for keys and intervals in any sequence of notes or chords. In this way, practice of motor skills literally increases motor vocabulary as well as dexterity and performance.

We live, think and imagine in movement.[7] Even our dreams are an internalised simulation of action.[8] The sense of *who* we are as effective physical beings in space begins with having a secure sense of *where* the body is in space. This sense, described by A. Jean Ayres as 'gravitational security', develops through movement experience alongside control of balance and posture in a gravity-based environment. The sense of 'body map' (knowing where different parts of our body are at any time) is a product of physical interaction with surroundings, which probably started before birth, continues with the seemingly random movements of the new born, develops into the more purposeful movements of the infant, and eventually becomes secure postural control and balance. Movement experiences help the developing child to understand where he/she is in space and where different parts of the body are in relation to each other. This physical sense of stability is not only important to learn to make spatial judgements but also provides a physical basis for emotional security.

Figure 1.1: Learning where my body begins and ends in space.

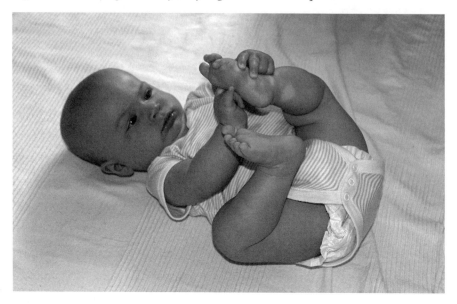

Figure 1.2: The sense of 'I'

Who am I?

= stability in space

• Structural Stability	Skeletal System
• CNS Maturity	Reflex System
• Balance	Vestibular System
• Bilateral Integration	Motor System

The product of a continuous process of synergy in functioning
of all position and motion sensors, structure and mechanics

Human infants make an incredible journey in the first year of life, from being a helpless prone or supine lying creature, lacking in muscle tone or control over voluntary movement, to upright posture. Achievement of secure upright posture releases the forelimbs and the hands from involvement in control of balance, and is one of the developments in our evolutionary past which enabled human kind to use tools and to develop spoken language; but language involves far more than the use of sounds to express thought.

Kohen-Raz, a doctor who spent a lifetime working in the field of specific learning disabilities and postural control, said that control of posture and independent use of the two sides of the body (particularly the hands) are precursors to fluent language development. When as a species we learned to stand on two as opposed to four feet, the ball of the foot took on the former function of the hands (front paws) in supporting balance and posture, making the development of lateral preference possible – an important factor in language development – as well as freeing the hands to develop the manipulative skills unique to humans.

The language of gesture precedes speech. If there is an impediment to verbal communication, human beings of every culture fall back on gesture as a means of making themselves understood. Gesture is a universal feature of human communication, although the nature and magnitude of gesture vary between cultures and languages (speakers of Romantic languages, for example, tend to be more physically expressive than speakers of Teutonic languages). A series

Figure 1.3: Quadruped to biped

of studies carried out in the 1980s point to a common brain mechanism for sequential movement and language[9] and it has been proposed that:

> … speech and gesture have their developmental origins in early hand-mouth linkages, such that as oral activities become gradually used for meaningful speech, these linkages are maintained and strengthened. Both hand and mouth are tightly coupled in the mutual cognitive activity of language. In short, it is the initial *sensori-motor* linkages of these systems that form the bases for their later cognitive interdependence.[10]

Adjacent areas of the brain involved in the control of rapid independent finger movements (dysdiadochokinesia) are also involved in control of the fine motor movements of the mouth used in human speech. Clinical observation of school-aged children who have difficulties performing rapid alternative movements with the fingers of one hand has found that these children consistently have a history of delayed speech, suggesting a neurological link between the motor pathways involved.

At birth, oral movements are primarily involved in feeding, but even at this early stage, there is a connection between movements of the mouth and movements of the hands and feet.

Human infants are equipped with a series of primitive reflexes, which develop during life in the womb, are active in the baby born at full term (40 weeks' gestation) and are gradually inhibited and integrated into more mature patterns of response, as connections to higher centres in the brain develop in the first six months of post-natal life. These early reflexes provide stereotyped responses to specific stimuli, are thought to help protect the infant in the first months of life, and provide rudimentary training for later voluntary skills. Early feeding provides an example of this.

Rooting and suckling reflexes develop during life in the womb. The rooting reflex is a reaction to touch to the area on either side of the mouth, which elicits nuzzling or searching with the face to locate the breast or bottle. As the mouth finds the nipple or the teat, contact with the roof of the mouth elicits suckling movements. Connected to these two oral reflexes are grasping reflexes in the hands (palmar reflex) and the feet (plantar reflex), which respond to touch applied to the palm of the hands, or pressure applied to the soles of the feet. In new-born infants, suckling movements of the mouth are accompanied by small grasping movements in the hands and the feet. This reciprocal link between hands, mouth and feet is sometimes stimulated if an infant has difficulty 'latching on' to the breast or bottle. Midwives may encourage the mother to apply pressure to the palms of the hands or soles of the feet, to elicit sucking movements. In this way, hands, feet and mouth are all involved in the sequentially timed movements of early feeding. Eventually this reciprocal link needs to be uncoupled in order to use hands, mouth and feet independently, but in the beginning all are involved in the motor experience of feeding and form part of the pattern of suck/swallow/breathe (SSB) synchrony, which will influence other areas of development.

Figure 1.4: Infant suck reflex.

The language of babies is also essentially musical, with the human infant (infant means 'one without speech') being a master of mime and song able to communicate mood, curiosity and response through a combination of cooing, babbling and gesture. Researchers at the University of Edinburgh have shown how, when analysed in slow motion, the apparently random arm movements of the infant resemble the highly expressive movements of an orchestral conductor, while mother–infant 'conversations'

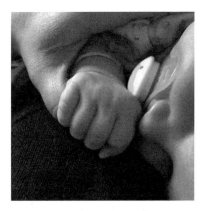

Figure 1.5: Grasping and sucking – the Babkin response

comprise perfectly shaped musical phrases comprising answering melodic sequences, rhythm and timing. These are the non-verbal, primal elements of language, which are universal in nature. They develop in the early years through a combination of trial and error, response and interaction.

The same researchers demonstrated how the desire to communicate using sounds is also dependent on having a sympathetic listener. Video footage was taken of mothers and infants engaged in conversation. When the mother used a short phrase and *waited* for her baby to respond, after a short pause the infant would respond with an answering melodic phrase, and this interaction could continue for several minutes. When an adult entered the room, spoke to the baby and then continued to talk without giving the baby time to respond, the baby looked away and any attempt at 'conversation' came to an end. Apparently babies understand manners rather well.

What Does Music Do?

Music as we understand it is thought to have developed from a combination of rhythms derived from the experience of movement (dance and marching rhythms, the beating of drums etc.) and sounds descended from the sounds of the natural world, including hunting calls, animal cries and bird song.

These two elements of music are primarily sensed by two components of the human ear – the vestibular or balance apparatus, which specialises in detecting changes in movement (rhythm) – and the cochlea, or hearing apparatus, which senses different frequencies of motion within a specific range (pitch). Paul Madaule, a psychologist who specialises in the treatment of listening problems, described the vestibular system as acting as 'the ear of the body', while the cochlea acts as 'the ear for sound'.[11] These two areas are particularly responsive to training, and while only a talented few will go on to become elite gymnasts, acrobats or musicians, every child needs to receive active stimulation of the two systems through physical interaction and experience to develop good control of balance, coordination and sound discrimination to support many higher skills, including language and, later, literacy.

Before the arrival of recorded music the notion of music involving action would have seemed self-evident because music is the expression not just of a series of sounds in space and time but the motor actions of the performer(s). It depends on the rhythmic measure of expressive movements in time.

> The architecture and narration of moving psychological time is manifested in the measured rhythms of human action, experience and communication, real or imagined – with its emotional qualities and their relation to human functions of the body.[12]

These are key elements of non-verbal language – the aspects of language which lend meaning, intention, emotion and colour to words – vital ingredients of effective communication. The musical qualities of language and how music contributes to language development will be explored further in Chapter 3.

Over the next chapters we will examine some of the origins and underlying mechanisms of movement control in the first year(s) of life and how music can be used to prepare the brain for language and literacy. How simple songs and stories can be used as the basis for movement activities which integrate sensory experience with thinking, and time spent developing the physical skills needed to support academic learning can reap rewards for the remainder of life.

In less advanced societies the instinct to parent is naturally passed down from mother and father to child through physical proximity and the close, shared experiences involved in daily living. Children partly absorb skills through 'modelling' the behaviour of those around them. Children are not shielded from the processes of birth, death and ageing, of hunting, gathering and preparing food, or of caring for younger siblings. These are a part of daily living. As societies have become more complex, so children are further removed from many of these natural processes so that they are ill-equipped to deal with aspects of life when they encounter them for the first time; in this context, in seeking to protect our children from harm we may actually being doing them a dis-service in terms of shielding them from acquiring the resilience needed to deal with real life events and processes.

Despite the many advantages of modern life from developments in medicine, which have eradicated many of the most feared diseases of childhood; education, which has opened up possibilities that were unimaginable for the majority of the population in former times; and technology, which has reduced the burden of labour and entertained and accelerated our ability to process vast volumes of information and access far flung parts of the universe at the touch of a button, the needs of the human infant and developing child remain relatively primeval. Effective learning does not just involve teaching from the top down, but also learning from the bottom up; it is a *process* in which each step along the way informs and secures the basis for later learning.

A system or society which forces young children into formal education and assessment too early, pushes them in one direction too soon, or focuses primarily on outcomes rather than processes, runs the risk of producing splinter skills – sometimes described as 'knowing of' versus 'knowledge' or 'know-how' – the latter being the result of experience combined with information, something which is understood from without and within, and enables children to apply known concepts to new situations, to solve problems and to be confident that they can adapt in a changing environment.

Of course children need to be taught how to read, write and use numbers. This is what schooling is for, but the seeds of these more advanced cognitive skills are sown and are cultivated slowly in the early years in the fertile ground of attachment, physical development, sensory processing and socialisation.

[1] Goddard Blythe, S A, 2005. *The well balanced child*. Stroud. Hawthorn Press.

[2] Stiles J, Jernigan L T, 2010. 'The basics of brain development'. *Neuropsychology Review,* 20:327–348.

[3] Rosselli M et al., 2014. 'Language development across the life span. A neuropsychological/neuroimaging perspective'. *Neuroscience Journal*, Volume 2014.

[4] Paynter A, 2006. 'Learn to move. Move to learn. St Aidan's School Partnership'. In *Inspiring Partnerships*. Youth Sport Partnership. www.youthsporttrust.org.

[5] Rowe N, 1996. Personal Communication.

[6] Hebb D, 1949. *The organization of behavior: A neuropsychological theory*. New York. Wiley and Sons.

[7] Dissanayake E, 2009. 'Root, leaf, blossom, or bole: Concerning the origin and adaptive function of music'. In: Malloch S, and Trevarthen C, *Communicative musicality. Exploring the basis of human companionship*. Oxford. Oxford University Press.

[8] Berthoz A, 2000. *The brain's sense of movement*. Cambridge MA. Harvard University Press.

[9] Ojemann G A, 1984. 'Common cortical and thalamic mechanisms for language and motor functions'. *American Journal of Physiology*, 246. (Regulatory Integrative and Comparative Physiology 15), R901–R903.

[10] Iverson J M and Thelan E, 1999. 'Hand, mouth and brain. The dynamic emergence of speech and gesture'. *Journal of Consciousness Studies*, 6/11–12:19–40.

[11] Madaule P, 2001. The Ear–Voice Connection Workshop. Chester.

[12] Trevarthen C, 2008. 'Human biochronology: On the source and function of 'musicality''. In Haas R and Brandes V, eds. *Proceedings of the Mozart and Science Conference*, Baden. October 2006. Vienna. Springer.

Chapter 2

Learning to Move, Moving to Learn

Origins of Movement in Infancy

The experience of movement is shared by all living things from sensing gravity derived from the earth's rotation on its axis, to hearing the birds sing. Different sensory systems – from balance to vision – comprise specialised groups of receptors which respond to different speeds or frequencies of motion. The characteristic of animate creatures is that they move from place to place; generally, the more varied and skilled the movement capabilities of the organism, the more complex is the nervous system needed to support them. An example of the relationship between movement and the nervous system can be seen in the case of the primitive Ascidian squirt. When it is young the Ascidian sea squirt swims from place to place, but as it approaches adulthood, it attaches itself to a rock and starts to behave more like a plant feeding itself by filtering passing plankton. When it becomes fixed to one place it starts to consume its own primitive nervous system, presumably because it no longer requires it. This is a reminder of the old adage that if you don't want to lose a function you need to keep using it, and this is just as important in infancy and childhood as it is in advancing age.

Berthoz[1] described how thoughts are an internalised simulation of action – the ability to visualise or imagine forms and relationships in the mind's eye – based on former movement experience. Even the word 'emotion' being derived from the word *emovere,* meaning 'to move', describes feelings which have a physical correlate in terms of the physical and chemical changes which occur and are associated with feelings of 'being moved'

Before birth, floating in amniotic fluid, supported by the structure and tissue of the mother's body and nourished via the placenta, the human fetus has been sheltered from the full force of gravity. From the moment of birth he/she must learn to breathe, feed and start to control his/her body in a gravity-based environment. On average, it will take twelve months for this apparently helpless creature, born comparatively early in gestation in relation to other mammals, to learn to stand on its own two feet. During this period the infant is equipped with a number of primitive reflexes, which initially help to support basic survival functions and are then gradually inhibited and integrated into higher (in terms of brain functioning) postural reactions that support posture, balance and coordination for the remainder of life.

Because the first year(s) are so important in laying the foundations for later skills, it is helpful to examine the role and development of certain primitive reflexes and postural reactions in the first three and a half years of life in the context of the interrelationship between nature and nurture,

The primitive reflexes can be categorised according to the two main types of stimulus that elicit the reflex response: reflexes which respond to change in position and reflexes which respond to touch.

Reflexes of Position

Reflexes of position are elicited as a result of stimulation to the vestibular system. The vestibular system is the sensory system that provides the leading contribution to the sense of balance and spatial orientation for the purpose of coordinating movement with balance. It is the main sensor of gravity and the first of the sensory systems to mature, being in place at 8 weeks after conception, functioning at 16 weeks and being the only one of the senses to be myelinated at birth. It responds to alteration of position – to turning, tilting, flexing or extending movements of the head or whole body in relation to the supporting base – and it senses when movements start, stop, alter speed or change direction.

The first reflex to respond to change in position, present at birth, is the Moro reflex. First described by Ernst Moro in 1918[2] – as a 'clasping reflex' – it is a reaction to sudden alteration of position, particularly position of the head in relation to the body, although it is also sensitive to sudden, unexpected stimulation of any of the senses. The reaction is immediate abduction (opening out) of the arms, the legs to a lesser degree, rapid intake of

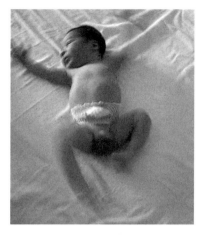

Figure 2.1: Moro reflex

breath and momentary 'freeze' in this position before the arms adduct (close in), and the baby exhales and starts to cry. At this early stage in development, the reflex acts as the infant's primitive fight/flight reaction and is accompanied by biochemical changes associated with fight and flight.

The phylogenetic meaning of this reflex is still unclear but it is thought to support survival in a number of ways. When activated it lowers the threshold of arousal, initiates a sudden intake of breath followed by exhalation, and in lower species probably enables an infant to cling on to its mother when afraid. In humans it is thought to provide a second fail-safe mechanism to stimulate breathing at birth, if breathing has not started spontaneously (there are various mechanisms and processes during a vaginal delivery which should prime breathing centres to function immediately after birth). It may also help to prevent suffocation in the first four months of life and summon assistance when the infant feels threatened.

It is inhibited (at 4 months of age) as connections to higher centres in the brain develop and is transformed into a more adult 'startle' response. Characteristics of the startle response are momentary startle, elevation of the shoulders, searching of the immediate environment for the source of startle followed by a conscious decision as to whether to react. The psychological difference between the two reactions is that whereas the startle response involves searching, identifying and then selecting a reaction pattern, the Moro reflex elicits a reaction first and a thinking response afterwards.

The absence of the Moro reflex during the neonatal period and early infancy indicates a variety of compromised conditions, while persistence of the Moro reflex beyond four months of age is generally considered to be a sign of lack of inhibition by higher brain centres. A persistent Moro reflex has also been found in adult patients suffering from agoraphobia, children with developmental delays and children with specific learning difficulties (SpLD's). Signs associated with a residual Moro reflex in the SpLD and adult population include hyper-reactivity and hyper vigilance to specific sensory stimuli, with secondary behavioural traits which can develop over time. In these same populations it has been observed that the reflex can remain reactive to specific stimuli if there is a fault in the functioning of a related sensory system.

Another reflex linked to position is the **Tonic Labyrinthine Reflex (TLR)**. This can be observed in the neonate if the position of the head descends below the level of the spine. This reflex divides the body from front to back in response to gravity so that if the neonate is suspended on his/her back or the head is placed in an extended position, gravity will pull the body into extension, resulting in increase in extensor tone in the body (Figure 2.2). Conversely, flexing the head forwards or holding the newborn horizontally on the tummy elicits increase in flexor tone (Figure 2.3). This reflex starts to be modified in its crude form from six weeks of age, as neck muscles, tonus and later head-righting reflexes start to develop, but it can still be elicited under certain conditions up to three and a half years of age, particularly when a child is learning a new skill. If atypical in an older child it can result in poor control and adaptation of muscle tone depending on head position, affecting balance, postural control and coordination. Later on, traces of the TLR can be linked to under-developed head-righting reflexes.

Head-righting reflexes are instrumental in providing a stable platform for centres involved in the control of eye movements, including gaze control. Retention of the TLR combined with under-developed heading-righting reflexes in the school-aged child can undermine control of the eye movements needed to support visual perception.

Figure 2.2: TLR in extension   *Figure 2.3: TLR in flexion*

While the primary mechanism for inhibition and integration of the TLR with other reflexes is neuro-developmental, in theory lack of movement opportunity in the first year(s) of life could also contribute to retention of infant patterns which are naturally integrated during the process of maturation. In other words, maturation of motor pathways is, in part, interdependent with activity and experience.

The **Asymmetrical Tonic Neck Reflex (ATNR)** is a response to turning the head to either side (lateral rotation). When the head is turned to one side the arm and the leg on the same side will extend and the opposite arm will flex.

Figure 2.4: ATNR – Just before the reflex is completely activated.

There is debate in academic and scientific circles as to whether this reflex should ever be considered physiological (relating to the way living things function), or is always a sign of pathology (indicative of deviation from normal), but the general consensus at the time of writing is that the ATNR is an involuntary 'attitude' (physical posture) prevalent at birth and in the first months of life, which is gradually modified as connections to higher centres in the brain develop. In common with other primitive reflexes, it never entirely disappears but is inhibited during the course of development to lie dormant in the brain stem, only to be released if there is accident or injury to higher centres, under conditions of postural stress, or if it is *voluntarily* released to assist in the execution of specific skilled movements.

Figure 2.5: ATNR released in the execution of skilled movement

www.myactivesg.com

In the first four to six months of life when the ATNR is activated, movement of the head, eyes, arm and hand are all linked together, which at this very early stage of development provides rudimentary training in eye–hand coordination. This is because the visual world of the new born is very different from the visual-perceptual world of the adult, and infants must learn how to use sight in combination with information from other sensory sources to support and develop visual perception.

In the first few weeks of life the infant is only able to focus at near distance; vision is blurred and the eyes are drawn to light, bright colours and outside edges rather than central features. When the ATNR is activated, the eyes move in the same direction as the head, following the movement of the arm, helping to extend baby's focusing distance from near point to arm's length and back again, and shifting visual attention between central vision and peripheral vision.

Near point   *Arm's length*

Figures 2.6 and 2.7: Hand–eye coordination with the ATNR

Within a short time, the extending arm will accidentally make contact with solid objects, and gradually through a combination of moving, seeing, touching, feedback derived from alteration in the tension of muscles, tendons and joints of the arm (proprioceptive feedback) and maturation of visual centres in the brain, eyes and brain start to learn how to adjust focus, distance and depth. In other words, what we understand as the adult sense of vision is a compound sense that has developed over many months and years through a process of sensory integration, partly entrained through the medium of movement, with the ATNR acting as a primary teacher in the first weeks of life.

If the ATNR remains active into later childhood it can impede balance, the ability to cross the midline of the body and hand–eye coordination when the head is turned to the affected side(s). The latter can restrict control of the hand when writing, affecting not only the ability to form letters and words and write at length, but sometimes also the ability to combine cognitive with mechanical processes when writing, interfering with the ability to transfer ideas on to paper in written form.

The Landau Reflex

Over time, primary reactions become modified either to disappear or to be progressively replaced by different reactions which evolve towards their final form. Others like the Landau reflex (three to seven months) and the Symmetrical Tonic Neck Reflex (STNR) are transitory and are thought to play an active part in modifying other primary reactions in the process of transformation from primitive reflex to flexible response.

The Landau reflex is elicited when a baby is held horizontally in the prone position and passive extension of the head leads to extension of the legs.[3] The extensor part of the reflex is thought to have a role in increasing extensor muscle tone in response to gravity, helping to modify the TLR in flexion (or the prone position) and develop muscle tone necessary to support posture and balance.

Figure 2.8: Landau Reflex

Symmetrical Tonic Neck Reflex

The Symmetrical Tonic Neck Reflex (STNR) is a normal response in infants to access the crawl position by extending the arms and bending the knees when the head and neck are extended.

Figure 2.9a: STNR in extension   Figure 2.9b: STNR in flexion

Initially when in the crawling position, if the head is flexed the arms also flex and the lower body tries to extend, making it impossible to maintain the crawling position and also move forwards using independent movements of the hands and the knees (Figure 2.9b).

Most babies will pass through a brief phase of rocking on hands and knees, which helps to integrate the reflex. If it persists, the infant might learn to 'bunny hop', bottom shuffle (Figure 2.10) or simply omit the crawling stage.

Figure 2.10:
Bottom-shuffle position

Figure 2.11:
Cross-pattern movement dragging one leg

In itself, failure to crawl is not abnormal, but in terms of forming neural connections, the process of crawling helps to integrate use of the visual, vestibular and proprioceptive systems in a new relationship with gravity; to initiate sequential cross-pattern movements (opposite arm and leg), which reflect and entrain interaction between the two sides of the brain (necessary for problem solving); and helps to train eye–hand coordination at a similar visual distance needed for reading and writing later on. In this way, different stages of motor development provide physical building blocks which support higher skills.

The knowledge or skills gained over time through trial, error and practice are very different from those acquired through passive stimulation. An infant given space and opportunity to learn 'how' to control his or her body in the physical world integrates physical learning with cognitive processes, so that they mutually support one another. This is quite different from being placed in a position and being entertained by electronic media (Figure 2.12).

Figure 2.12: Example of effect of baby seats on physical exploration and mobility

www.athomechildcare.co.nz

Reflexes Elicited by Touch

The sense of touch develops before all other senses in embryos, and is the main way in which infants learn about their environment and bond with other people. While the vestibular system and proprioception (a branch of the tactile system) provide *internal* information concerning the body's position in space, hearing, vision and smell inform about *external* stimuli, and the sense of touch tells us where we begin and end as individual beings in the physical world. The sense of touch provides the boundary to the physical sense of self.

Touch enables an individual to determine an object's size, shape, weight, texture and temperature, and whether the contact is a source of pleasure or pain. While the mechanics of how touch is transmitted to the brain are the same, the touch experiences of an individual through the life-span are unique and will affect the developing architecture of the brain, and how that person will interpret and respond to touch – the individual's 'story'. How this story develops is a two-way process in which the type of touch a person receives will shape how they tolerate and respond to touch, but the personal response to tactile sensations will influence how much they seek out touch.

Affectionate touch is necessary for the physical, mental and emotional development of children. In the first half of the twentieth century doctors became aware of a syndrome prevalent amongst children in hospitals and orphanages in which children failed to thrive, despite receiving adequate medical care, nutrition and hygiene. Harry Harlow's studies in which he separated monkeys from their mother and siblings at birth, providing them with clean cages and adequate food but depriving them of physical nurturing, showed how primal and how strong is the need for touch in young mammals. In addition to those placed in clean cages with access to food, he set up another group, also separated from their mothers, but provided with two 'dummy' mothers covered with terrycloth to make them soft. The infants would ignore the desire for food and cling to the terrycloth mothers, demonstrating that the need for affectionate touch transcends even the desire for food. The infant monkeys who had only had access to feeding started to engage in behavioural abnormalities similar to those associated with distress or psychiatric illness in humans, such as self-clasping, repetitive rocking and presenting as emotionally lame. They showed little interest in their environment or in socialising with other monkeys, and were timid and disliked being touched. When they did interact they were aggressive, and as they matured had difficulty in finding sexual partners, were often unable to mate properly and were abusive to their partners and offspring.

Not only in childhood, but also in adult life, lack of affectionate touch contributes to depression, memory deficit and the onset of illness. This is an increasing problem amongst a progressively ageing population in which ageing brings social isolation and a cessation of the daily touch experiences which keep us in contact with the world. Increasingly, it is recognised that the sense of 'self' is shaped and defined in the context of relationships.

Early touch experience also enables a child to 'read' the body language of another. One of the insidious trends in modern technological societies is an ever-increasing degree of physical separation from the natural world. In less so-called 'advanced' societies, where mother and child are in close physical proximity for the first nine months of life, physical closeness engenders a natural empathy. In one tribe where it is common practice for the infant to be strapped to the mother's body during the day for the first few months of life, the concept of nappies would be viewed as extraordinary. The mother is so attuned to her baby that she can sense when the baby needs to urinate or defecate, and she simply lifts the baby off her body and positions him/her over the ground. It is considered a source of shame if she fails to recognise her child's need in time. Physical communication between care-givers and child enables a child to understand the mood of others through the nature and quality of handling he/she receives.

Affectionate touch lowers stress and anxiety levels affecting not only mood and motivation but also the functioning of the immune system and the regulation of the hormones which act as the chemical messengers for both the nervous system and emotional stability. Hormonal dysregulation can have an effect on growth, immune functioning, mood and memory.

The tactile system receives several types of sensation from the body – light touch, pain, pressure, temperature, and joint and muscle position (proprioception) – but these different types of touch are organised into three different pathways in the spinal cord and have different targets in the brain:

- *Discriminative touch*, which includes touch, pressure and vibration
- *Pain and temperature* including the sensations of itch and tickle
- *Proprioception* (internal) relating to muscle stretch, joint position, tendon tension, etc.

The central nervous system must rely on five sensory nerve receptors in the skin to keep it informed about its environment. These receptors are: light touch (surface), pressure (deep), temperature (hot & cold) and pain. It is quite possible for one type of receptor to be hyper or hypo sensitive and the other normal. This explains why some children may tolerate light touches, but dislike firm hugs; or hate labels in clothes, or having their hair or nails cut, but seek activities which involve deep pressure sensation. Practitioners of Sensory Integration (SI) – a specialised branch of occupational therapy – talk about modulation in sensory functioning being the key to well-being.

Issues relating to hyper- or hypo-sensitivity to touch can persist through childhood into adult life-affecting relationships as well as behaviour. Hyper-sensitive individuals may not want to hug or hold hands with their partners, may seem undemonstrative and aloof in their relationships, avoid situations that involve close physical contact and prefer talking to touching. Socially, children who are hypo-sensitive to touch can have difficulty recognising physical boundaries, tend to invade the personal space of others, have a compulsive need to touch things, are not aware when they hurt themselves, have dirty hands or have a runny nose and seek out robust physical activities, often with very little sense of danger.

The first manifestation of response to touch emerges at five to seven and a half weeks post conception (pc). Initially the reaction – an amoebic-like movement of the whole body away from the stimulus (withdrawal) – is to stimulation in the area around the mouth. Gradually, areas responsive to touch become more differentiated, spreading to the palms of the hands and the soles of the feet, until eventually the entire body becomes reactive.

As the fetus matures, the withdrawal response changes as primitive reflexes that respond to touch develop. These include the plantar, palmar, rooting suck and spinal Galant reflexes. The palmar and suck reflexes are grasping responses, the plantar reflex is a protective reaction and the spinal Galant reflex is an avoidance reaction.

Both the **palmar and plantar grasp reflex** can be elicited in all normal preterm infants at as early as 25 weeks of postconceptional age.[4] Routine ultrasound examination has shown fetal palmar grasping of the umbilical cord from as early as 16 weeks' gestation.[5] Both reflexes can be elicited in infants during the first three to six months of age, decreasing thereafter with the intensity of the responses, usually disappearing by six and 12 months of age respectively.[6, 7]

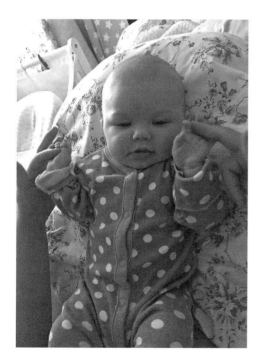

Figure 2.13: The Palmar reflex

The palmar reflex is elicited by placing an index finger into the palm of the infant and applying light pressure. The response comprises flexion of all the fingers around the stimulus, starting with finger closure with the thumb underneath and leading into clinging.

The **plantar reflex** is elicited by applying pressure (thumb) against the sole of the foot just behind the toes. The response is flexion and adduction of all the toes.

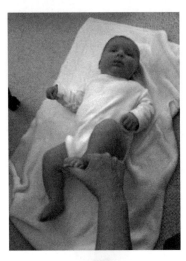

Figure 2.14: The Plantar grasp reflex

As infants develop, maturation of (higher) cortical connections overrides the generators of primitive reflexes in the spinal cord and brain stem, leading to the disappearance of the primitive reflexes and the emergence of righting and equilibrium reactions.[8, 9] The transformation of these mechanisms has been demonstrated to be chronologically related to the attainment of motor milestones.[10]

An example of this relationship can be seen as the palmar reflex decreases and manual dexterity increases. There are many stages involved in this process and environmental influences on inhibition of the palmar reflex probably include using the hands to support weight when placed in the prone position (Figures 2.15, 2.16 and 2.17) and the process of learning to 'let go' of an object. The reflex is normally elicited when pressure is applied to the palm, but the process of supporting upper body weight using the forearms probably also has an inhibitory effect.

Figure 2.15   *Figure 2.16*   *Figure 2.17*

The next step is to learn to release an object at will, which develops after the infant has learned to sit and the hands become less involved in supporting posture. While adults quickly get bored of the game of picking up an object their baby repeatedly drops, babies delight in the process of releasing a toy, seeing it fall, waiting for someone to hand it back, grasping and dropping it again. The ability to let go is a precursor to being able to form a 'pincer' grip and independent movement of the fingers and thumb necessary for fine motor control in the hands. Retention of the palmar reflex beyond the first year of life has implications for manual dexterity and related skills, including the mechanical aspects of handwriting.

There can also be a connection to speech via a reciprocal link between the hands and the mouth, active in infancy. The **Babkin reflex** is an additional response to stimulation of the palms comprising reflex-opening of the mouth and flexion of the arms. It can be elicited from the time of birth, becomes increasingly suppressed with age and is inhibited by the end of the fifth month.[11] Persistence beyond the fifth month is generally regarded as abnormal. The reflex is sometimes used to encourage feeding in the early weeks of life if an infant is unwilling to feed or to latch on. Pressure applied to the palms will cause the mouth to open; when the nipple or teat makes contact with the roof of the mouth, suckling ensues. The same link can be observed in hand-reared young mammals separated from their mother – when they suck on a bottle, they make kneading movements with their paws. Starting out as a hand–mouth reflex, as control of non-primary motor cortices over the reflex mechanism increases, it evolves into the voluntary eye–hand–mouth coordination needed for food intake.

The significance of this hand–mouth connection, if it persists, is that it can interfere with the development of *independent* hand-from-mouth movements, which also reflect the functioning of associated areas in the brain.

Figure 2.18a:
The Babkin reflex

Figure 2.18b: The Babkin reflex seen in an infant engaged in non-nutritive sucking

What is the significance of the hand–mouth relationship and why might this be linked to speech?

- Gesture and referential pointing precede speech (mime). Pointing involves the ability to separate movement of the index finger from the thumb.

- Freeing of the hand from postural control and locomotor functions allows the development of manipulative skills, which are thought to have had an important role in the evolution of language.

- The mouth and hand are two related movement systems that start out coordinated with one another (early feeding), but must become uncoupled for the development of fluent speech and independent manipulative skills.

- Adjoining areas of the brain are involved in fine motor control of the fingers and in fine motor control of the lips and tongue (Figure 2.19)

- Hands, mouth and feet are all involved in early babbling (Figure 2.20)

- Areas involved in language (Broca) are also activated during motor tasks[12] and when visualising motor tasks.[13]

- Older children (above six years of age) in whom hand and mouth movements remain coupled often have difficulties with fine motor skills (handwriting), control of rapid alternating movements in the fingers (dysdiadochokinesis) and a history of earlier speech-related problems.

- Speech (oral culture) precedes use of written language in both evolution and child development. Speech problems can be associated with later difficulties with aspects of written language, including reading and spelling.

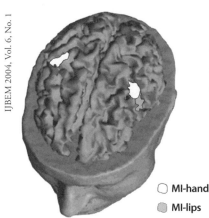

Figure 2.19: Adjoining areas of the brain involved in movement of the hand and the lips

○ MI-hand
◐ MI-lips

It is not only the hands but also the feet that are involved in early infant vocalisations. Rapid movements of both momentarily precede babbling, as if the motor pathways involved are 'gearing up' in preparation for vocalisation. Just as hand and mouth movements must gradually become uncoupled to work in cooperation, so, as the feet become involved in control of upright posture and locomotion, feet and mouth movements also need to become autonomous. Disappearance of the plantar reflex is related to voluntary use of the feet for standing.

Figure 2.20: Hands, mouth and feet all involved in early babbling

If the plantar reflex persists into later childhood it can result in postural instability from the base, as involuntary gripping with the toes alters the main point(s) of weight distribution and flexibility in the feet. Some children may try to avoid eliciting the reflex by 'toe walking' thereby distributing weight forward of the point at which the reflex is stimulated.

Rooting and Suck Reflexes

The rooting reflex begins when the corner of the baby's mouth is stroked or touched. The baby will turn his or her head and open the mouth to follow and search or 'root' in the direction of the stroke (Figure 2.21). This enables the baby to find the breast or bottle and prepare to feed. Rooting activity may be difficult to elicit in a baby who has recently been fed, but become urgent and insistent in a hungry infant.

Figure 2.21: The Rooting reflex

When the roof of the baby's mouth is touched, stimulation of the suck reflex will initiate sucking. This reflex is not functional until about the 32nd week of pregnancy and is not fully developed until about 36 weeks. Consequently, premature babies may have a weak or immature sucking ability resulting in a combination of sucking issues, which may include:

- Disorganised or inefficient sucking patterns
- Weakened lip seal
- Impaired tongue shaping or movement
- Weakened stability of the inner cheek
- Trouble synchronising the suck and swallow with breathing
- Infant Respiratory Distress Syndrome (RDS).

Babies with RDS have difficulty synchronising their sucking, swallowing and breathing, making it difficult to withstand long feeds and tiring easily. This can sometimes affect weight gain and nutritional status.

Figure 2.22: The Suck reflex

Around two to three months of age, sucking will become a conscious function and no longer be a reflex response. Sucking is also a soothing, enjoyable experience, and expedites bonding and social activity for babies.

'At birth the mouth exhibits the most organised neuromotor behaviour available to the infant.'[14] We have already seen how the sense of touch is the earliest to show signs of response, beginning with the area around the mouth, with sucking and swallowing patterns being well established by 15–18 weeks gestation.[15] The value of this mechanism for nutrition and survival is obvious, but the rooting and suck reflexes also initiate responses towards the stimulus for interaction and exploration. Peiper[16] observed that the tactile response leads into visual recognition, so that eventually sight of the breast or bottle will be sufficient to initiate sucking movements.

The primary mechanism developed through oral-motor activity is suck/swallow/breathe synchrony (SSB).

> It is the first developmental pattern that requires timing and sequenced movements. An intact synchrony is critical to many elements of sensorimotor and cognitive development including speech and language development, state regulation, postural control, feeding/eating behaviour, ego development and eye-hand coordination.[14]

In nutritive sucking, as soon as the stimulus is inserted into the mouth the suck reflex makes the infant clamp down on the breast or bottle, establish a seal and squeezing, or in the case of breast feeding stripping milk from the breast, with the sucking action creating a vacuum. The tongue moves the fluid to the back of the tongue until there is enough to stimulate a swallow. This process needs to be well synchronised with a pause for breath to allow respiration without aspiration. This complex process, combined with development of tone in the muscles of the cheeks, jaw and lips, developed over time through the action of sucking/swallowing and breathing will support the timing and fine motor movements needed for progressing to solid foods, drinking and speech later on.

Older children who develop specific problems with speech production often have a history of prolonged feeding problems (difficulty chewing, or avoiding certain consistencies or textures) or copious dribbling (indicative of poor lip seal). These problems are not necessarily related to early neuromotor function but can also develop as a result of structural anomalies as well as enlarged tonsils or adenoids or nasal congestion, any of which affect the position of the tongue in the mouth, SSB synchrony and lip seal.

Non-nutritive sucking (fingers, dummy etc.) regulates arousal levels and in so doing affects brain-wave activity, which parallels different levels of attention. Sucking is thought to help develop control of eye movements involved in near-point convergence, as well as providing different training for the timing of swallowing and breathing needed to support speech. In this way, rooting and suck reflexes lead the way into the development of more mature SSB patterns, but equally, if early oral reflexes persist then the SSB pattern can remain immature. In this way, primitive reflexes act as one of the very first lessons, which lead into the development of more complex skills, but children should not remain 'stuck' on the first lesson.

Spinal Galant Reflex

The **Galant** reflex, or truncal incurvation reflex, is a newborn reflex, named after neurologist Johann Susmann Galant.[17] It is elicited by holding the newborn face down (ventral suspension) and stroking along one side of the spine. The normal reaction is for the newborn to laterally flex towards the stimulated side. Sometimes the head will also turn towards the same side (Figure 2.23).

If both sides are stroked or stimulated simultaneously from the pelvis to the neck, the **Pulgar Marx reflex** is elicited resulting in 'flexion of both legs, lordosis of the spine, elevation of the pelvis, flexion of the arm, lifting of the head, loud crying culminating in apnoea and cyanosis, emptying of the bladder and relaxation and bulging of the rectum with bowel movement; after the reflex has fully developed there is general hypotonia

Figure 2.23:
The Spinal Galant reflex

Originally published in: Reflexes, Learning and Behavior. Fern Ridge Press. Eugene.

lasting for several seconds.'[18] Not all of the features of the reflex are present every time it is activated. It is inhibited by two to three months of age.

Little is known about the functions of the spinal Galant reflex, although it has been suggested that it may take an active role in the birth process. When humans as a species learned to stand on two as opposed to four feet, bipedalism resulted in a problem in the design of the existing human birth canal. Because of the shape of the female pelvis, the baby has to work its way down the canal in a spiral motion making two 90° turns along the way. Contractions of the vaginal wall during the second stage of labour stimulate the lumbar region, potentially eliciting the spinal Galant and Pulgar Marx reflexes within the confines of the birth canal, eliciting small rotational adjustment in the hips on either side, and/or lordosis of the spine after the head is born. In this way, although the baby is often referred to as the 'passenger', in a natural vaginal delivery mother and baby work together as cooperative partners in the birth process. The spinal Galant reflex may be just one of many mechanisms that assist in this process.

It has also been suggested that the Galant reflex may act as a primitive conductor of sound in utero, facilitating sound vibrations to travel up through the body in the aquatic environment of the womb enabling the fetus to 'feel' sound.[19] Some weight has been added to this hypothesis by a study carried out by a speech and language therapist and physical therapist using a method of sound therapy (Auditory Integrative Training – AIT) for the treatment of various listening- and language-related problems. In assessing evidence of residual primitive reflexes in this group before and after treatment with AIT, Butler Hall (1998) found that the only reflex which *consistently* responded to treatment (decreased) was the spinal Galant reflex, suggesting that there may be a functional relationship between hearing and the spinal Galant reflex.[20]

The Galant reflex may also be a hangover from a time earlier in evolution when humans had a tail. Useful for mammals that use tails for balance, support and species-to-species signalling, the tail is missing in apes and in humans. However, all human embryos initially have a tail. Normally, they regress into four to five fused vertebrae (the coccyx). The Galant reflex is present in infants through the period of quadruped locomotion (crawling on hand and knees), recedes as the infant progresses to standing and walking, and should have disappeared by two years of age. As long as it remains, it can be elicited at any time by light pressure to the lumbar region. A stimulus to *both* sides of the spine can activate the Pulgar Marx reflex if it is still active, resulting in involuntary urination. A residual spinal Galant reflex is often seen in older children who continue to wet the bed regularly after the age of five.

Another long-term effect of the spinal Galant reflex can be difficulty sitting still. Because the lumbar region remains sensitive to touch, changing pressure or movement, the reflex can be aroused by shifting sedentary position, leaning against the back of a chair or alteration of pressure from the waistband of clothing. This sensitivity and reaction can be like an intermittent source of interruption affecting not only the ability to sit still, but also to concentrate. I used to describe having one such child in the house as being like having a bluebottle flying in the room!

Postural Reflexes

Postural reflexes emerge after birth and may take several months to develop, depending on the type of reaction involved. The transition from primitive reflex to postural reaction is not an automatic one with set times at which one reflex 'replaces' an earlier one. Rather, the pattern of reflex integration in the first year of life is like a complex interweaving spiral (Figure 2.24) in which earlier and later reflexes can co-exist for a short period of time. Once developed, most postural reflexes should remain for life unless accident, injury or degeneration intervene.

Postural reflexes fall into two main types: *righting reactions* – reflexes that through various receptors, in labyrinth, eyes, muscles, or skin tend to bring an animal's body into its normal position in space, and that resist any force acting to put it into a false position, for example, on its back; and *equilibrium reactions* – reactions which appear after righting reactions have developed, which are compensatory in nature and available to modify righting reactions. It is not the purpose of this book to provide a detailed description of all the reactions involved, but rather to provide the reader with a 'taster' of several reactions, to gain an understanding of how maturation and experience work together to support postural development.

Postural control develops as a *general* head-to-toe and centre-outwards process, mirrored in the emergence and practice of various postural reactions. Mature postural reflexes function collectively rather like an efficient secretary to the executive part of the brain, supporting control of balance, posture and coordination just below the level of consciousness.

The first task a child must accomplish is mastery of head control. This tends to be gained in the prone position before supine, with the infant being able to hold its head in line with its body for a few seconds by six weeks of age (Figure 2.25). By 12 weeks he/she can lift the head above the general body line and maintain control for several minutes (Figure 2.26). Developing head control is accompanied by increase in muscle tone so that by twelve weeks the legs are no longer flexed and the pelvis is flat on the surface when lying prone (Figure 2.27). By 16 weeks, he is able to press down with his forearms to lift his head and upper torso, stretching his limbs and appearing to 'swim' in this position (Figure 2.28).

The gradual sequence of developing head control in the first two to four months of life heralds the development of two sets of **head-righting reflexes:** *oculo* head-righting reflexes – which respond to visual cues – and *labyrinthine* head-righting reflexes, which respond to gravity. Together, these head-righting reflexes ensure that the head maintains a midline position in relation to the supporting base, despite movement to, or of, other parts of the body. In other words, when the body is displaced the head should make an equal and opposite adjustment to the displacement of the body. Sometimes described as *vertical righting reactions,* these reflexes are elicited so that the head can right itself in relation to prone, supine, lateral and eventually sitting and standing positions (Figure 2.29).

In addition to establishing a secure relationship between position of the head in relation to the supporting base, from which other muscle groups can make adjustments to maintain control of balance, ability to keep the head level

Figure 2.25: Head control in prone position at circa 6 weeks of age

Figure 2.26: Head control in prone position circa 12 weeks of age

Figure 2.27: Head control and increased extensor tone at 12–16 weeks

Figure 2.28: Head control in prone position circa 16 weeks of age

Figure 2.29: Head-righting reflex in sitting position

Figure 2.30: Under-developed head-right reflexes affecting eye control

against gravity provides centres involved in the control of eye movements, with a stable platform or reference point from which to operate. Under-developed head-righting reflexes can affect control of eye movements, as can be seen in the slightly younger child where head-righting reflexes are not yet fully developed in the sitting position (Figure 2.30).

Head-righting reflexes develop first in prone, then supine, quadruped, sitting and eventually standing positions. Time and opportunity to learn 'how' to control the head in relation to the body combined with practice help to develop strength as well as confidence in space and problem solving. Generally speaking, the more time and space children have for physical exploration, the better the related skills will become.

Other postural reflexes such as the Amphibian and Segmental Rolling reflexes develop to facilitate independent movement between different parts of the body and fluency in sequential movements.

The **Amphibian** reflex emerges at four to six months of life, appearing first in prone and then in supine. Elevation of the pelvis on one side elicits flexion from the hip to affect the knee on the same side (Figure 2.31).

Figure 2.31: Amphibian reflex on the right side in a five-month-old baby

Flexion of one leg irrespective of head position reflects the increasing ability to carry out independent movements in each quadrant of the body, and reflects significant reduction in the influence of the ATNR. It will later make possible crawling on the tummy.

Segmental Rolling reflexes are a later modification of earlier reflexes which align the trunk with the head when either is rotated or turned, but the segmental rolling reflexes are strictly rotational reactions. These reflexes, which emerge from six months of age, facilitate rolling, usually starting from supine to prone at six months, followed by prone to supine from eight to ten months, followed by sitting, four-point kneeling and eventually standing. They are activated from two key positions in the body: the shoulders and the hips. Movement starts at the head, then follows to the shoulders, thorax and pelvis or vice-versa. As the child becomes more adept at these activities, the reflex becomes partially redundant and in later life a variety of rolling patterns may develop.[21] The development of sequential rolling patterns enables movement instigated in one part of the body to follow through in a sequential pattern, enhancing fluency of performance and reducing effort. These patterns will later support many gross motor activities such as running, jumping, skiing etc. Once again, time spent on the floor with opportunity to learn *how* to roll helps to develop and support a range of later skills.

Not all of the primary reflexes associated with the first year(s) of life have been covered in this chapter, and there are other reflexes which have a protective function and persist in adult life, including:

- Blinking reflex – blinking the eyes when they are touched or when a sudden bright light appears.
- Cough reflex – coughing when the airway is stimulated.
- Gag reflex – gagging when the throat or back of the mouth is stimulated.
- Sneeze reflex – sneezing when the nasal passages are irritated.
- Yawn reflex – yawning when the body needs more oxygen.

[1] Berthoz A, 2000. *The brain's sense of movement*. Cambridge, MA. Harvard University Press.

[3] Moro E, 1918. Das erste Trimenon. *Münchener Medizinische Wochenschrift*, 65:1147-1150.

[3] Thomas A et al., 1960. *The neurological examination of the infant*. Medical Advisory Committee of the National Spastics Society, London.

[4] Allen M C, Capute A J, 1986. The evolution of primitive reflexes in extremely premature infants. *Pediatric Research*, 20/12:1284–1289.

[5] Sherer D M, 1993. Fetal grasping of the umbilical cord at 16 weeks' gestation. *Journal of Clinical Ultrasound*, 12/9:316.

[6] Futagi Y, Suzuki Y, Goto M, 1999. Clinical significance of plantar grasp response in infants. *Pediatric Neurology*, 20/2:111–115.

[7] Zafeiriou D I, 2000. Plantar grasp reflex in high-risk infants during the first year of life. *Pediatric Neurology*, 22/1:75–76.

[8] Molnar G E, 1978. Analysis of motor disorder in retarded infants and young children. *American Journal of Mental Deficiency*, 83/3:213–222.

[9] Blasco P A, 1994. Primitive reflexes: their contribution to the early detection of cerebral palsy. *Clinical Pediatrics*, 33/7:388–397.

[10] Milani-Comparetti A, Gidoni E A, 1967. Routine developmental examination in normal and retarded children. *Developmental Medicine and Child Neurology*, 9/5:631–638.

[11] Futagi Y, Yanahihari K, Mogami Y, Ikedi T, Suzuki Y, 2013. The babkin reflex in infants: clinical significance and neural mechanism. *Pediatric Neurology*, 49/3:149–155.

[12] Bonda et al., 1994. Cited in: *Perception and Action. Recent advances in cognitive neuropsychology*. Decety, Jean (Ed). 1998. Psychology Press.

[13] Krams et al., 1998. Cited in: *Neuroimaging in clinical populations*. Frank G. Hillary and John De Luca (Eds). London. Guildford Press.

[14] Oetter P, Richter E W, Frick S M, 1989. *M.O.R.E. Integrating the mouth with sensory and postural functions*, 2nd edition. Hugo MN. PDP Press.

[15] Ianniruberto A, Tajani E, 1981. Ultrasonographic study of fetal movements. *Seminars in Peritanology*, 5:175–181.

[16] Peiper A, 1963. *Cerebral function in infancy and childhood*. New York. The Internataional Behavioral Sciences Series.

[17] Oetter et al., as note 14.

[18] Galant S, 1917. *Der Rückgratreflex: ein neuer Reflex im Säuglingsalter mit besonderer Berück-sichtigung der anderen Reflexvorgänge bei den Säuglingen*. Doctoral dissertation, Basel: Basler.

[19] Pulgar Marx I and De Marx P De, 1955. *Rev. Espan. Dedlat.* 113–117; see also *Zentralb Kinderheilk*, 58:220, 1957.

[20] Dickson V, 1991. Personal communication. Cited in S.A. Goddard, 2002. *Reflexes, learning and behaviour*. Eugene OR. Fern Ridge Press.

[21] Butler Hall B, 1998. Discovering the hidden treasures in the ear. Paper presented at the 10th European Conference of Neuro-Developmental Delay in Children with Specific Learning Difficulties. Chester. UK. March 1998.

[22] Crutchfield C A, Barnes M R, 1993. *Motor control and motor learning in rehabilitation*. Atlanta, GA. Stokesville Publishing Company.

Chapter 3

Nursery Rhymes for Modern Times

The sense of hearing starts to develop before birth, with babies showing signs of response to external sounds from as early as the 24th week of pregnancy. Because the fetus is enclosed in a water-filled sac and protected from the outside world by the mother's body, the experience of sound is very different from how we understand it. Sounds heard in the womb are felt as vibrations conducted through the media of water and bone (after birth, sounds are primarily sensed through air conduction), with internal sounds of the mother's body providing the dominant acoustic environment interspersed with the episodic over-riding melody of her voice. Her voice provides an acoustic bridge between pre-natal and post-natal life, acting as 'the primary medium by which mothers coax their babies into the human cultural world'.[1]

Only a narrow range of sound frequencies can be heard from within the womb, the spectrum of sounds being approximately equivalent to the range covered by classical musical instruments and the possibilities of the human voice. Sounds are muffled and are primarily musical in nature: the beat of the mother's heart, the pace of which will vary according to emotional and physical changes; the background rumblings of her digestive system and pumping of her circulation. These provide the background or underlying harmony to the melody, phrases and cadences of her speech.

I met Russian physician and musician Dr Michael Lazarev in 2002 at a conference held at the University of Derby where he was giving an introduction to the musical training programme he had developed for the unborn child (SONATAL) and I was talking about the use of a developmental movement programme based on replicating infant movements in school-aged children (INPP school programme). We both recognised the developmental parallels between our two areas of work – the use of music as sensory stimulation affecting all levels of the brain, and movement to entrain brain–body connections, both providing physical foundations for physiological and emotional regulation and precursors to verbal language.

At an early stage in his work, Lazarev had realised that the prenatal communication possibilities between mother and her unborn child are not a passive process determined simply by the gene code or a period of waiting until after birth, but are active before birth. One way in which the unborn child can help to be prepared for life is by harnessing the innate and universal language capabilities of the unborn child – the ability to feel the 'music of language' and to experience the language of movement – using musical communication between parents and child starting before birth and continuing up to the age of seven.

The mother's voice is a particularly powerful teaching instrument, because during life in the womb her voice will have been felt, first through vibration and later through low- and medium-frequency sound as part of the self. Lazarev describes the biological union of mother and unborn child using the Russian word 'Mamalyish'. There is no adequate translation for this term in English, but it describes mother and child as a single being. When a pregnant woman uses her voice, her body acts as a resonator like the sound board of a stringed instrument, stimulating the entire cellular system of the developing child. He has written a series of songs and musical activities for parents to use from pre-birth up to seven years of age, with studies in Russia showing improved functioning in the immune systems, motor and later scholastic development of children who have been raised on the system. To understand why these simple songs and poems can support children's development in the early years, it is helpful to know some of the rationale that lies behind them.

His system evolved in the quest to find a solution to two puzzles:

- What principal factors influence a baby before birth?
- How is it possible to communicate with babies before birth through the mother?

Lazarev wrote:[2]

> Mankind appeared some 50 million years ago and during this time man has undergone considerable evolution: first he learned to stand (circa two million years ago; then he learned to act consciously (circa 100,000 years ago) and finally during the last 15–10,000 years he developed into man as we now know him.
>
> Anthropology data show that during the course of this evolution significant changes have taken place in body proportions, height, weight, duration of life, intellectual abilities etc. But the most important factor during the course of evolution has been the corresponding changes that have taken place in life environment, with this environment becoming the engine, determining the activity of contemporary man from the moment of birth.
>
> On the other hand the environmental conditions of the fetus before birth have changed much less. He still grows inside the uterine cavity, surrounded by amniotic fluid listening to the beat of his mother's heart. In other words, a baby passes from ancient pre-birth conditions into a totally new environment in which he must learn to adapt to increasingly complex social conditions.
>
> Neurophysiologists recognise that at the moment of birth the human brain has already lost some of its neurons. If these neurons did not have a purpose, nature would presumably have already discarded the excess earlier in development in the same way it relieved us of a tail, leaving only the rudiment as a coccyx.
>
> Does this mean that while evolution continues to increase the neuronal potential of man (more than 100 billion cells), mankind does not actually use it? In other words, the human baby, having already lost some of his neuronal reserve by the time of birth, enters the 'noosphere' deprived of the

totality of protective and adaptive resources evolution provided for him, and is instead forced to cope with the increasing demands of modern life furnished only with the reserves, which belonged to his ape-like ancestors. Is this an underlying factor in contemporary problems of the human condition such as drug addiction, violence and self-destructive behaviour? In other words, while evolution has prepared prenatal reserves for the brain, man does not use them. This renders the infant less able to cope with the sensory overloads and developmental demands needed to 'catch up' with modern civilisation. In compensation, he starts to turn to unnatural stimulants or substitutes to continue to support function in an increasingly stressful world. It is no mere chance that many psychologists have called the 21st century the century of dependencies and addictions.

How can we help to optimise the neuronal potential of the unborn child and socialise his environment to prepare him for entry into the noosphere? My method started with the search for an answer to this question.

Before birth, although the baby is protected from many external environmental stimuli, he still experiences many of them in a different way. One of the main sources of external stimulus is sound. Sound stimulates development of the prenatal brain, and for nine months of prenatal life the child, subject to acoustic influences, experiences the primary elements of socialisation. How can we optimise this potential?

Here my colleagues and I had a revelation. It appeared that this natural process did not require invention or acquisition of something new because the mother's voice, accompanied by special touches and motions, is the natural process of social prenatalization. This occurs in the context of the 'Mamababy' experience, the physical, physiological and sensory world provided for the baby and shared by the dyad of mother and child. The most important element of prenatalization is the physical activity of the Mamababy.

This raises a further question. Is it necessary for the language of communication to be strictly national or is there the possibility of elaboration of universal prenatal speech which prepares a Mamababy for the universal perception of the world and communication with it, not limited to one language?

Although Lazarev goes on to say that the Russian language is particularly useful in this respect because it encompasses one of the widest ranges of sound frequencies used in spoken languages, music is a universal form of language containing all the non-verbal aspects of speech and communication: melody, intonation, rhythm, beat, cadence, phrasing, key modulation and emotion. Therefore, music delivered to the unborn child through the medium of the mother's voice is also a powerful means of communication and socialisation.

Others have also recognised that learning to listen begins before birth. In an article 'Sounding out dyslexia' published in *World Medicine* in 1977, Colin Tudge described how:

> In effect, a newborn baby has already had three months' hearing experience, albeit muffled, but probably similar to a 60-decibel conductive hearing loss. From about the third month of life (that is, after six months hearing experience) he seems to develop a memory for pitched sounds – to respond appropriately to the clatter of spoon on plate and to the pitch and tone of his mother's voice.[3]

He went on to say that when a child is learning to speak, he does not simply copy but produces his own sounds de novo, of exactly (or near enough) the right quality and intensity to constitute convincing words, beginning with the vowel sounds, which are different one from another only because of the differences in their dynamics; in high-pitched frequencies that overlie the fundamental tone, and then developing an auditory memory; 'a repertoire of sounds that can be vocalised at will, so that you know in your head what a word sounds like and can say it'. It seems that the most sensitive period for developing pitch discrimination occurs as a result of experience in the first year(s) of life.

While it is often thought that musical ability runs in families and must therefore have a genetic component, exposure to musical sounds in the early years probably also plays an important part in fostering musical potential. My father was a professional classical musician, who tutored my mother at the piano when she was expecting me. As I worked my way through the various piano grades as a child, the pieces I really wanted to play were the ones that had been in her repertoire during the months she was expecting me, although I had no conscious memory of having heard these pieces before. She also used to quiz me to guess who the composer of a certain piece of music was when it was played on the radio. This taught me how to listen for the 'signature' of the composer which can usually be heard within a single chord or notes of a piece. This sound signature is like the colours, use of light and brush technique of an artist, from which the trained eye can identify the hand.

Learning to hear these subtle differences from an early age helps to develop not only pitch discrimination but also understanding of mood, character and meaning. In a similar way, the daily experience of following my father up the spiral stairs to the organ loft of college chapel every weekday morning on my way to nursery school, and sitting in the organ loft while he played the morning service, has given me a life-long love of organ and choral music. I have no doubt that for me, this early exposure to the sounds of classical music prepared me for the sounds of language, and has had a life-long influence on how I write.

The ability to discriminate pitch fades during childhood so that by the sixth year, the size of the pitch change needed for discrimination becomes increasingly larger (less sensitive):

> The standard eventually achieved in pitch discrimination appears to be controlled by the age at which pitch became 'meaningful', and training available, and the finest standards are reserved for those who had appropriate experience during the first years of life. In our visually orientated society we simply allow the potential for perfect pitch learning to abort.[4]

Lazarev has written thousands of songs for children at different ages and stages, and in the music that he has written has a remarkable ability to 'tap in' to the developmental needs of the child. I witnessed an example of this when I was working with families in Poland through a translator a number of years ago. Half way through the day (and a consultation) the translator, without warning, left to take her lunch break. I was left trying to communicate with a family who spoke no English with a little boy of 6 years of age diagnosed on the autistic spectrum. As I tried to fill the silence while we waited for our translator to return, I started to play one of Lazarev's songs – 'The Crocodile' – a song rich in vocal low frequencies and a funky rhythm, which makes you want to move in time with the music (remember that music developed from movement). The boy spontaneously went down on to the floor and started to crawl across the room on his tummy in time to the music, although he had no idea that the words of the song were about a crocodile. In other words, implicit in the rhythms, modulations and melodic phrases that he writes is the timing of corresponding movement patterns. Lazarev's songs encourage children to want to sing along and to move with the music.

Why is singing along relevant? When a child follows the line of a tune or another singer, he is not a mere copyist; in the process of vocalising he is also 'sounding out' tonal variations and speech sounds which will support language and literacy for life. The ability to understand language is as good as the ability to differentiate where one word ends and the next one begins, similar to the experience of visiting a foreign country and hearing an unfamiliar language being spoken for the first time. Initially, when listening to local people in conversation it sounds like a meaningless stream of sounds with alterations only in tone, stress and volume. As we attempt to speak a new language, firstly using single words usually accompanied by gesticulations to add meaning to what we are trying to say, then short phrases, so we gradually start to separate elements from the general stream of sounds. In other words, by *speaking*, translating sounds into a series of muscle movements needed to articulate and practise those sounds, the ability to 'hear', understand and eventually pronounce them improves. Probationary choristers go through a similar process when first joining a cathedral choir.

When one of my sons was admitted to the choir, the master of choristers said that the reading age of all his choristers improved by twelve months within six months of joining the choir, irrespective of whether they were good or poor readers at the time of joining. His explanation was that in the process of singing they were 'reading' material far in advance of their actual reading age, and this accelerated reading skill. While this may be the case, there is probably more to the 'mixture' than simply reading. Much of the material children in a cathedral choir sing is in complex liturgical language, far in advance of their actual reading ability, or it may be in other languages including Latin. At this stage, they do not 'read' the words, but put the sounds of language to music, following the voices of more senior choristers alongside them. As they initially sing 'by ear', putting words to music, the ability to match visual symbols on the page to the sounds being produced improves.

In this way, singing enables children to start practising the sounds of speech without having to read or 'think' about what they are going to say first. In imitating sound patterns through song, the ear, the voice and the brain are all trained. French ear, nose and throat specialist A. E. Tomatis said that the voice can only produce what the ear can hear, but the ear is continually renewed and entrained through use of the voice via 'the audio-vocal feedback loop'. This occurs not only as a result of sound transmitted to the ear through air, but also through vibration and bone conduction conveyed by the jaw to the ear. Both the jaw and the ear (including the balance mechanism) developed from the same embryonic tissue, which originated from the spaces between the gill bars in fish.

Vocal organs are controlled by a more primitive part of the brain than areas which control speech and language. Self-voicing not only provides feedback to the ear but provides training in matching sounds to motor output, listening and copying, and enables us to 'feel' emotion, meaning and intent through the tonal variations, timing and stresses involved. Because singing can only be done using 'open' sounds, extra time value is given to vowels, with consonants acting as the start/stop points, rather like a natural form of punctuation. In effect, singing slows down the sounds of speech, making it easier to hear and articulate individual sounds and patterns involved.

Unlike visual symbols, auditory information is transient and must be memorised. Initiating speech involves the acquisition of auditory memory, a repertoire of remembered sounds and sound sequences that can be vocalised at will. Voicing helps not only to practise sounds, but also to embed them into memory.

Wings of Childhood brings together for the first time the musical talent and paediatric knowledge of Michael Lazarev with the developmental work pioneered at The Institute for Neuro-Physiological Psychology (INPP). In 1996, I had developed a short screening test and developmental movement programme for teachers to use in schools.[4] The former comprised a few simple tests to enable teachers to identify children in whom immature neuromotor skills may be playing a part in educational performance/achievement; the latter, based on a clinical programme used at INPP, put together into a movement programme designed to be used in schools as a class-based activity under teacher supervision every day for one academic year. The movements involved replicate normal stages of infant motor development, the theory being that not only do the movements reflect maturing systems in the brain, but the movements themselves help to form efficient neural pathways which support many other areas of functioning. The screening test and movement programme have been the subject of a number of pilot projects and published research, which has shown that:

- There is a relationship between immature neuromotor skills and lower educational performance.

- Children who participated in the INPP developmental movement programme showed increased maturity in neuromotor skills compared to control and comparison groups.

- There was a small improvement in a test for non-verbal cognitive skills in children who took part in the programme.

- In children who had both immature neuromotor skills and a reading age below their chronological age at the outset, children who followed the daily movement programme showed increased improvement in measures of neuromotor maturity and educational performance.[6]

The song collection in *Wings of Childhood* can simply be enjoyed as a delightful collection of songs for children to sing along with parents – a series of new nursery rhymes for modern times. It can also be used as the basis for music and movement activities, encouraging children to act out through movement the 'characters' and stories of the songs. The animal characters have been specially selected based on developmental principles of movement and can help to prepare children for more advanced skills later on.

The songs have been recorded using bass and soprano voices to provide a wide range of sound frequencies. Children should be encouraged to sing along with the songs. The second part of the CD contains a charming medley of piano solo improvisations on the songs, to which children and parents can add their own words and movements. This is an activity for fathers as well as mothers (Lazarev stresses that the father's voice is just as important as the mother's in encouraging pre- and post-natal communication), and can be used in nursery and pre-schools settings.

[1] Panksepp J, Trevarthen C, The neuroscience of human emotion. In: Malloch S, Trevarthen C (Eds), 2009. *Communicative musicality. Exploring the basis of human companionship.* Oxford. Oxford University Press.

[2] Lazarev M, 2007. *Mamababy.* Moscow. Olma Media Grupp.

[3] Tudge C, 1977. Sounding out dyslexia. *World Medicine*, 19 October 1977:33–36.

[4] Tudge (see note 3).

[5] Goddard Blythe S A, 2012. *Assessing neuromotor readiness for learning. The INPP developmental screening test and school intervention programme.* Chichester. Wiley-Blackwell.

[6] Goddard Blythe S A, 2005. Releasing educational performance through movement. A summary of individual studies carried out using the INPP test battery and developmental exercise programme for use in schools with children with special needs. *Child Care in Practice*, 11/4:415–432.

Chapter 4

Wings of Childhood
Songs by Michael Lazarev. Illustrations by Sharon Lewis

This chapter contains the words to the songs performed on the CD 'Wings of Childhood' together with suggested activities to accompany the songs.

The song collection can be enjoyed simply as a delightful collection of songs for children to sing along to with their parents, while playing alone or sitting in the car. It can also be used as the basis for music and movement activities at home, in nursery or reception classes, encouraging children to act out through movement the 'characters' of the stories.

The animal characters have been specially selected based on evolutionary and developmental principles of movement. Practice of early stages of movement helps to strengthen neural pathways between the brain and the body and prepare children for more advanced motor, rhythmic, listening and sequencing skills later on.

The songs have been recorded using solo bass and soprano voices to cover a wide spectrum of sound frequencies and to mimic the voices of mother and father. As explored in previous chapters, research has shown that a child's listening environment in the first two to three years of life provides the sound basis for speech, language and reading later on. According to Tomatis we read with our ears, by developing an 'inner voice' which eventually is able to read words silently while 'hearing' a voice inside the head.

Children should be encouraged to sing along with the music (whether in tune or not!) because use of the child's own voice radiates sounds internally (bone conduction) and externally (air conduction), strengthening the sensory input of sounds produced. Use of the self-voice helps to train sound discrimination and encourages development of the 'inner voice' internalised through feedback and practice.

The second half of the CD comprises a charming medley of piano improvisations on the songs, to which children, parents and teachers can add their own words, movements and stories. In this way, the CD is intended to provide the basis for creative as well as structured play.

Instructions for Using the Songs and Movements:

1. Listen, hum along and dance to the songs.
2. Sing the songs with your child until your child can remember the tune and some of the words.
3. Get down on the floor and show your child the movements that match the songs.
4. Use the CD for singing and movement games.
5. Tracks 11–22 have the accompaniment only. These can be used as the basis for movement activities, or for you and your child to sing along with.
6. You and your child can develop your own movement activities as your child becomes competent at carrying out the suggested movements – suggested movements are only a guideline to start with.

Wings of Childhood

A New CD of Nursery Rhymes for Modern Times

1.

Sea Anemones

Beautiful anemones, crimson, purple, blue
Living in the ocean gloom
Waiting just for you.
Moving they linger
Spreading ev'ry finger.
Swaying and fluttering
Twisting and dancing.

Catching fish they cower
That's what they devour.
Creatures of the seas,
Living little weeds.
Playing ev'ry hour,
Shining sea-bed flowers.

Creatures of the seas,
Living little weeds.
Playing ev'ry hour,
Shining sea-bed flowers.

Exercise

Lie on floor on the back.
Curl up into a ball with the
arms and ankles crossed
(like a flower closing its petals).

Slowly, uncross the arms and legs,
stretching out the fingers.
Let the hands and feet
sway and twist in the air
from the wrists and ankles.

Curl up into a ball again.

Repeat in time with the music.

2.

The Turtle

The turtle is sitting in his thick armour
His head to shoulders stuck.
The turtle is crawling in his thick armour
Slowly crawling up.

His head is turning and he's looking,
Just above his shirt of armour.
Squeaking heavy shirt of armour
Crackling heavy shirt of armour.
His neck moving very slowly
It's rememb'ring some great show.
It's rememb'ring some great show
Some old show
That no one knows.

Repeat both verses once more.

Exercise

Crouch on the floor on hands
and knees.
Like a turtle, close to the
ground, with head tucked
down.

Slowly lift the head up
Like a turtle crawling out from
under its shell.

Move the head up and down,
Slowly turn it from side to side.

Slowly start to move forward,
Lifting and turning the head
while slowly creeping forward
in time to the music.

3.

Caterpillar

In the garden, when I stroll,
Many caterpillars crawl.
Lady with a tummy,
Caterpillar's Mummy.
Near-by running water,
Is caterpillar's daughter.

Lady with a tummy,
Caterpillar's Mummy.
Near-by running water,
Is caterpillar's daughter.

Caterpillar, caterpillar
Green leaves' royal princess.
Caterpillar, caterpillar
Garden's fairy tale.

Caterpillar, caterpillar
Delicately minces,
Caterpillar, caterpillar
Wiggling its fat tail.

Repeat Verses 3 and 4 once more.

Exercise

Lie on the tummy, forehead
resting on the floor.
Slowly tilt the head up until the
back of the head is in line with
the body.
Pause.
Slowly lower the head down
to the ground. Repeat the
movement a few times.

When the rhythm of the song
starts to change (caterpillar,
caterpillar… etc.), slowly wriggle
across the floor in time with the
music.

4.

Lizard

A greenish little lizard
Is quickly looking round.
Her greenish little eyes
Examine what they find.

Eyeing quickly what she's seen,
Proudly like a mighty queen
Her head turning
She keeps looking all around.

Eyeing quickly what she's seen
Proudly like a mighty queen
Her head turning
She keeps looking all around.

Scuttling feet with fun and cheer
She shows up and then she disappears.
Through the grass she scampers on,
She quickly rushes.
Tiny beetles flee away from grass and bushes,

Running on and running on and
Running on and running on and
Running on and running on and running on.
Repeat last three lines once more.

Exercise

Lie on the tummy.
Quickly move the head
from side to side.
Repeat a few times.

Raise up on to the hands
and knees.

Stand up and scamper
around the room in
time to the music in the
second part of the song.

5.

Crocodile

Green crocodile
Green crocodile
Green crocodile
Green crocodile

Green crocodile he stalked
Along the bank he walked
Along the bank, along the bank
Along the bank he walked.
Along the bank, along the bank
Along the bank he walked.

Repeat verse one once.

Picked flowers near the bogs
Played hide and seek with frogs.
Played hide and seek, played hide and seek
With merry croaking frogs.
Played hide and seek, played hide and see
With merry croaking frogs.

Repeat first verse to fade.

Exercise

Lie on the tummy.
Slowly crawl across the floor
using opposite arm and leg,
keeping the tummy in
contact with the floor all the
time.
(Like a crocodile crawling
through the mud).

Try to keep hand and foot
placement in time with the
music.

6.

Peacock

How beautiful a peacock is!
What a big and shiny train!
Give me, peacock, give a quill, oh please!
It is like a sunny rain.
What a fantastic glow.
This is a real show.
Mister Peacock, hello
You are the best, I know.

What a fantastic glow
This is a real show.
Mr Peacock, don't go
See my respectful bow.

Exercise

Stand with feet together,
knees slightly bent,
head held high,
arms by the sides.

Slowly open out the arms in
a big, wide circle, reaching up
until the hands meet above the
head (as if fanning the tail).

Move the arms up and down
as if 'showing off' the tail while
strutting around the room.

7.

The Bear

Prowling thro' the forest
Big and furry bear.
He's picking pine cones
And he's singing there.

Prickly little pine cones
Quickly slipped away.
Made him very angry
Stamped his foot, growled 'Hey!'

Prowling thro' the forest
Big and furry bear.
He's picking pine cones
And he's singing there.

Stomp, Stomp, Stomp, Stomp
Stomp, Stomp, Stomp, Stomp

Exercise

Go down on to hands and knees.
Slowly stomp forwards,
placing opposite hand and knee
on the ground in time to the
music.

8.

Deer

The deer is little
But he has strong horns.
When he grows bigger
His foes will be scorned.

Legs will gain velocity
Antlers gain ferocity
Delicate like tracery
Magic trees of lacery.

Over snow he'll gallop
Looking for his luck,
The deer, the deer, the deer
Legs that never tire
Chasing the sun's fire.
The deer, the deer, the deer.

Racing, frolicking, playing
Antlers gently swaying.
He'll go, he'll go, he'll go.

His hooves softly kicking
He moves thro' the drifting of snow;
Of snow, of snow.

Clip clop clip,
The deer will run.
All day long
He'll chase the sun.
Antlers never growing tired
Giving him the pace of fire.

Repeat above final verse once.

Exercise

Stand, alert and poised as if
ready to move (like a young
deer).
Turn the head from side to
side as if sniffing the air.

When the music speeds up,
gallop and frolic around the
room in time to the music.

9.

The Stork

The stork a great flyer will beat,
In the air, the air, the air, the air.
And then it goes higher
Like wind it goes higher
Than flares, than flares, than flares

I'll ask the good stork, oh please make me a flyer,
Oh people aren't flyers I know.
I'll ask the good stork, oh please make me a flyer,
How quickly my wings will then grow.

I'll ask the good stork, oh please make me a flyer,
Oh people aren't flyers I know.
I'll ask the good stork, oh please make me a flyer,
How quickly my wings will then grow.

Exercise

Free expression
of movement as
suggested by the
words of the song.

10.

Butterflies

With wings of the butterflies
Fields are a-glitter,
In summer
The beautiful butterflies flitter.

From flower to flower
They merrily fly
Winking with a wing's colourful eye.

They hide their bright wings
From the winter time freeze.
They dream of the summer
And cry for warm breeze.

The wish for the snow to be gone very soon
And the meadows will be covered with
flowers in bloom.

Exercise

Stand with arms outstretched.
Wave the arms up and down
like butterfly wings.

On tip-toe,
gently run around the room,
waving the arms, pausing
as if to rest on a flower for a
moment and then, flying on.

Chapter 5

Early Morning by the Pond

Lazarev's songs and the stories in the next two chapters all follow the principles of normal infant movement development, providing activities to encourage children to practise, through play, stages of emerging postural control, starting from a prone or supine lying creature to rolling, sitting, crawling, standing and running. Each of the following stories and suggested activities are based on programmes developed at The Institute for Neuro-Physiological Psychology (INPP) in Chester.

INPP was originally set up in 1975 by psychologist Peter Blythe with three aims:

1. To investigate whether specific learning difficulties (and agoraphobia and panic disorder in adults) were linked to immaturity in the functioning of the central nervous system (CNS).
2. To develop reliable methods of assessing maturity in the functioning of the CNS in children and adults.
3. To develop effective remedial programmes using physical exercises.

Since 1975, INPP has assessed and supervised remedial programmes for thousands of school-aged children. Some of those children had received a prior diagnosis of a specific learning difficulty such as dyslexia, developmental coordination disorder (formerly dyspraxia), attention deficit disorder or the mild end of the autistic spectrum; others were simply under-achieving. Using evidence of residual primitive reflexes and/or under-developed postural reactions (aberrant reflexes) as indicators/signposts of immaturity in the functioning of the central nervous system (CNS), individual movement programmes have been prescribed for them, which were carried out at home every day under parental supervision. The developmental movements involved replicate earlier stages of infant development, thereby giving the brain a 'second chance' to inhibit and integrate earlier primitive patterns and develop more mature ones. As posture, balance and reflex profile mature, corresponding improvements take place in control of the eye movements needed to support reading, writing, copying, spelling, catching a ball etc., as well as hand–eye coordination and the ability to sit still. These individual programmes were designed to be used with children from seven years of age and upwards. They should not be viewed as a 'cure' for any underlying disorder, but rather as training regimes, which facilitate more efficient communication between the brain and body, based on Hebb's principle of neurons which fire together, wire together. Children remain on the individual programme for approximately twelve months, during which time the movements are done every day, progress is reviewed at 6–8 weekly intervals and the programme of exercises adjusted accordingly.

Whilst individual programmes are effective in improving motor skills of school-aged children presenting with various problems, there is also a growing number of children who are entering the school system with inadequate motor and language skills to meet the demands of the classroom and the curriculum and realise their potential. At the time of writing, few researchers are willing to point to a single cause for this increase, which is probably multifactorial. However, there is much that could be done to *prevent* children entering the school system under-equipped in terms of their motor and language skills. Much of the theory to support this has been outlined in previous chapters – *Early Morning by the Pond* and *A Day in the Garden* are just 'starter' ideas to help parents encourage their children to actively participate in listening and moving. Although many of the movements are similar to formal exercises used in an individual clinical programme carried out under the supervision of a trained practitioner, the stories, songs and suggested activities are designed as *informal* play for younger children (3–6 years): they should be used as part of daily story-telling and play, and should **not** be regarded as therapy.[1]

By harnessing natural movements in a developmental sequence, improved coordination tends to become an integrated function rather than simply a practice learned skill. (Skills that are dependent on continuous practice tend to lack flexibility and do not necessarily adapt or transfer to new situations.) The majority of suggested movements to accompany aspects of the two stories are carried out on the floor, starting with movements designed to develop correct head alignment with the body (the basis for good posture), and the ability to use the two sides and upper and lower sections of the body in different ways (the basis for coordination).

Underlying Principles of Motor Development

Movement development during the first year of life follows a general chronological course starting from the head to the toe (cephalo-caudal) and from the centre outwards (proximo-distal). Development on the tummy is usually more precocious than development on the back, provided the infant has had opportunity and experience of 'tummy time' in the first year.

Children gradually progress from movements which involve the whole body to more differentiated movement. The first step is being able to hold the head up and isolate head movement from movement of the rest of the body. In the first six months an infant also learns how to bring its hands and eyes to the midline and to cross the midline from side to side. This is essential for later development of fluent cross-pattern movements.

Control of the balance between flexor and extensor muscle tone begins with control of the head and gradually works down towards the trunk, but also from the feet upwards. Truncal rotation, which develops in the second six months of life, facilitates increased fluency by linking one stage of movement to the next into sequential movements (chain reactions). All of this should have taken place before a child is ready to crawl on hands and knees. One of the major differences between the INPP individual programme including the play-based activities suggested here for younger children, and many other motor training programmes such as Brain Gym, Sensory Integration (SI), Activate etc. is that the INPP movements take children back to the *beginning* of balance training working through a developmental sequence.

Sensory-Motor Development

Development of the senses also follows a sequential pattern in the first year of life.

While the sense of touch is the earliest to show signs of response, the first sense to become fully operational is the sense of balance. Formed at just 6–8 weeks after conception, functioning at 16 weeks, balance is the only one of the sensory systems to be myelinated at the time of birth in a full-term baby. After birth, the infant must learn how to use the sense of balance in cooperation with other senses. This is rather like a child being bequeathed a grand piano at birth but the piano will remain silent or only yield discordant notes, unless the child learns to play and improve performance *through regular practice.*

Immature balance is often linked to generalised 'gravitational insecurity'. Gravitational security is the product of having a secure sense of position in space and is important not only for physical coordination but also for certain cognitive skills. The balance mechanism was described by Levinson as acting like an internal compass system, providing crucial information concerning position of the self in space (internal), from which spatial judgements (external) are formed. Children with poor balance often struggle with situations which involve making spatial judgements, such as invading other people's personal space, judging the time and speed of approaching objects, directional problems such as difficulty telling the difference between left and right, putting clothes on the right way round, seeing the difference between similar letter and number shapes such as b and d, 5 and 2, s and 5, and so on. Even the ability to tell the time using an analogue clock is rooted in spatial awareness, to differentiate up and down, left and right, before and after, etc.

Developing alongside the sense of balance is the sense of touch. Information derived from touch helps to affirm the sense of balance in its interaction with the environment. Children can be hyper- or hypo-sensitive to different types of touch (deep or light pressure, for example). Exercises that are carried out on the floor provide plenty of tactile input, while the floor provides a secure base from which to control movements of the body, thereby helping to improve integration in the functioning of the vestibular and tactile systems.

Proprioception is enhanced by carrying out movements as slowly as possible, providing deeper proprioceptive sensation to the muscles, tendons and joints than if a movement is carried out rapidly. Young children can find it difficult to perform movements slowly. If this is the case, allow them to repeat each movement several times at their own pace. Slowness can be encouraged when reading parts of the story aloud, the narrator setting the pace for the accompanying movements through *use of the voice* to mimic the actions of the characters in the story. This should also increase the enjoyment for parent and child in the story-telling, as well as making it easier to hear all the phonological components of the words.

The role of the visual system in learning is so essential that it may seem remiss not to include specific visual training in an early movement programme. In contrast to balance, hearing and proprioception, vision, dependent on light to function optimally, only starts to become fully functional after birth. Although vision develops rapidly in the first weeks of life, the foundations for oculo-motor functioning and visual-perceptual skills are inextricably linked to the functioning of the balance mechanism, postural control and motor development in the first months and years of life. By developing the latter three (and provided there are no primary visual problems), the functional foundations for ocular-motor development are laid.

Many children can compensate for deficiency in control of balance provided they can use vision to tell them where they are in space; but compensation demands a price elsewhere, and such compensatory use of the visual system can lead to 'overload' or visual stress, resulting in difficulty processing multiple visual stimuli or rapid coding of visual information. Subsequent related difficulties might include figure–ground effect (difficulty differentiating foreground from background), potentially affecting visual attention and perception.

Behavioural effects of this can superficially seem bizarrely unrelated to control of either balance or vision, and result in avoidance of situations that require these systems to function well together. Adults with figure–ground problems describe experiencing extreme fear and avoidant behaviour when having to cross a slatted bridge where they can see the gaps between the planks, with the effect that the two visual distances *appear* to be in competition. The associated feelings were beautifully described in a poem 'Cold Feet' by Brian Lee (opposite).[2]

Other visual-perceptual problems associated with functional immaturity in the two systems can include poor depth perception, erratic visual pursuit movements (smooth eye-tracking movements are vital to follow a line of print when reading, without loss of place) and the ability to adjust focus rapidly over different visual distances (accommodation). Good visual skills involve far more than simply eyesight – there really is more to vision than meets the eye.

Using the Stories and Movements Together

Basic movement patterns have been broken down into their simplest form and rebuilt step by step following a developmental sequence. With the exception of standing activities, all are based on normal infant movement patterns, acquired during the first six to nine months of life.

If children experience difficulties with early exercises, spend more time on these before moving on to later ones. You can still progress with the story, so that the child becomes familiar with what is coming next, but more time is spent on developing fluency in the early movements.

• Start off either by playing the narrated story on the CD or by reading as much of the story as holds your child's interest.

• Play or read again a section of the story which accompanies the first exercise(s).

• Ask the child to imagine they are the character in the story.

• Demonstrate the accompanying exercise.

• Ask the child to carry out the exercise as shown:

  1. First of all, as if in slow motion.

  2. Repeat several times slowly.

  3. Repeat two to three times a little more quickly.

Cold Feet

by Brian Lee

They have all gone across
They are all turning to see
They are all shouting 'come on'
They are all waiting for me.

I look through the gaps in the footway
And my heart shrivels with fear,
For far below the river is flowing
So quick and so cold and so clear.

And all that there is between me and it
And me falling down there is this:
A few wooden planks – not very thick –
And between each, a little abyss.

The holes get right under my sandals.
I can see straight through to the rocks,
And if I don't look, I can feel it,
Just there, through my shoes and my socks.

Suppose my feet and my legs withered up
And slipped through the slats like a rug?
Suppose I suddenly went very thin
Like the baby that slid down the plug?

I know that it cannot happen
But suppose that it did, what then?

Would they be able to find me
And take me back home again?

They have all gone across
They are all turning to see
They are all shouting 'come on'
They are all waiting for me.

- Return to the story and instruct children to carry out the movement again while listening to the story, matching their movements to the appropriate part of the story. If reading yourself, try to inject the 'timing' you want for the movements into your telling of the story.
- If your child is too young to follow the timing of the story, or only wants to play at being certain characters, use this as a free play time with the child developing his/her own movements.

If using the stories with older children in a nursery or reception class setting, remember that key components of the programme are *regularity, repetition* and *duration*. In order to derive benefit from either of the stories or the music CD, ideally the activity needs to be carried out on *several days of the week, every week* during term time *for one academic year.*

Please note: if you have any concerns about your child's physical development, please check with your health visitor before carrying out any daily programme of exercises.

If your child is currently receiving treatment for a related disorder, check with your consulting physician or therapist before using any of the suggested exercises.

1. Busy Bee

Busy Bee was hungry and he knew from the sweet smell of pollen coming from the flowers in the early morning sun that it was time for making honey. He buzzed around in circles in excitement, following the scent of the biggest, brightest flower until he felt quite dizzy.

He stopped, closed his eyes and rested on the flower. He let the giddiness stop and then anxious not to let anyone else get to the best flower before him, he took off and circled around in the other direction until he settled on the next flower.

He stopped again, this time drinking in the warmth of the sun and feeling of pollen tickling his back.

Suggested Exercises and Movements:

Standing Activity

- Stand with arms outstretched to the sides.
- Turn around a few times in one direction.
- Close the eyes and stand still until the feeling of dizziness stops.
- Open the eyes and turn around in the opposite direction.
- Close the eyes and stand still until dizziness stops. Always turn an equal number of times in each direction.

2. Christopher the Caterpillar

Christopher the Caterpillar was asleep under
a big leaf in the early morning sun. As the
warmth of the sun started to creep under the
leaf, Christopher slow... ly lifted his head
up a little way to greet the day.

(He kept his eyes firmly shut
because the sun was so bright, and
he really was very sleepy.)

He paused for a moment and
wondered whether he should go
back to sleep.

A big drop of dew rolled off the lead on to his head.

'Oooooh!', he thought, 'that shower was very cold, and I don't remember
turning the tap on. I am definitely going back to sleep' (because he did not
want to wake himself up any more by doing anything too quickly). He let his
head lower down to the ground again.

'Bother!', he thought, 'my bed is
all damp now. I can't get back to
sleep. I suppose I should see who
left the tap on upstairs

Slow... ly, he lifted his head
up a little way again. He was
still very sleepy and his head felt
very heavy.

'Mmmm', he thought, 'perhaps if I can sleep for a little longer, my head
will get lighter' and slow... ly, he let his head drop to the ground again.

Meanwhile... On the other side of the leaf...

Suggested Exercises and Movements:

Floor Movements

- Lie on the tummy, head resting on the forehead, arms bent at either side.
- Slowly lift the head a little way off the ground until the back of the head is in line with spine.
- Pause.
- Slowly lower the head on to the forehead again.

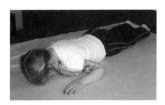

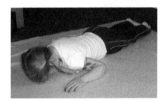

Floor Movements

- Lift the head up again. Open the eyes, turn the head from side to side and look around a little.
- Close the eyes and lower the head.

3. Flossie the Flower (Part 1)

Flossie the Flower was getting ready
to start her day.

She had spent the
night all curled up
inside her petals, which
wrapped around her
like a warm blanket.

As the sun got up,
slow… ly, she started
to uncurl her petals and stre… tched her head back so that she could feel the
warmth of the sun on her face.

'Oh what a love… ly start to the day', she thought, 'I could spend all day
just following the sun across the sky'.

A big grey cloud started to cross the face of the sun.

'Oh, it's cold!', she thought to herself. 'I need some more clothes on', and
slowly, she started to wrap her petals around herself, and tried to tuck her nose
inside her petals so that it would not turn red with the cold and make her look
foolish in front of the other flowers.

The cloud moved across the sun, and the sun smiled down on her again.

'This is better', she thought. 'I have a busy day ahead.'

Slow… ly, she stretched open her petals again, determined that this time,
no cloud was going to spoil her day.

Suggested Exercises and Movements:

Floor Movements

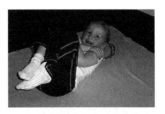

- Lie on the back, knees off the ground, arms crossed and feet crossed at the ankles.
- Chin tucked in towards the chest.
- Slowly let the head tip backwards until the back of the head is resting on the floor. Uncross the arms and legs and open out. (Keep the arms and legs slightly flexed.)

- Pause.
- Slowly curl up into the starting position.
- Tip the head back, and uncross the arms and the legs again. Repeat sequence 2–3 times.

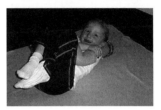

4. Flossie the Flower (Part 2)

Flossie opened out her fingers
and toes, waited for a
moment, then curled
them up feeling the mud
of the early morning
squishing between
them.

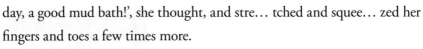

'Aah, just what a
girl needs to start the
day, a good mud bath!', she thought, and stre… tched and squee… zed her
fingers and toes a few times more.

While Flossie was enjoying her mud bath…

Suggested Exercises and Movements:

Floor Movements

- Let the head rest on the floor. Arms by the sides and legs straight. Place both hands so that the palms of the hands are resting flat on the floor.
- Splay the fingers and toes (child may need help in spreading the toes). Relax and repeat several times.
- Curl the fingers into a tight fist and curl the toes. Pause and repeat several times.

5. Christopher the Caterpillar

Christopher the Caterpillar
was seriously thinking
about getting up.

Slow… ly, Christoper
raised his head a few more
times, keeping it just under
the leaf, because he did not
want any more unexpected
showers.

This time he felt a little braver. He
lifted his head, stre… tched his neck and supported himself with his front legs.

'Thank goodness someone has turned the tap off', he thought.

Another big drop of dew fell down from the leaf.

'This is too… much', said Christopher. He
was now feeling very cross.

He started to push (kick) up and down
with his back legs. He wanted to move
out of the damp place where his bed
had been, but the dew had made his
bed all muddy, and he kept getting
stuck

In the pond…

Suggested Exercises and Movements:

Floor Movements

- Lie on the tummy.
- Lift head a little way.
- Push up supporting the upper body on the forearms (elbows stay on the ground).

Floor Movements

- Lower head and upper trunk to the ground.
- Lift one leg off the ground, bending at the knee. Change legs.
- Continue alternate slow kicking movements with each leg.

6. Bertie the Beetle (Part 1)

Bertie the Beetle was floating on his back.

It was not the most comfortable position for a beetle to be in, but he had been searching for something and somehow rolled over and got stuck that way. A gentle breeze was wafting him across the pond but he felt he should try to help himself.

Slow... ly he stre... tched one of his front legs (arm) back behind his head and straightened it. The stretching felt so good, he stretched a little further. Then he brought his arm down and did the same thing with the other arm.

'Ooh', he thought, 'I'm swimming – I didn't know I could swim.'

7. Bertie the Beetle (Part 2)

Bertie carried on for some time until he thought he was near the edge of the pond. He stopped swimming because he was afraid he might hit his head on the bank.

Slow... ly, he lifted his head up to see how far he was from the other side. He had to do it several times before he knew how much further he had to go.

Suggested Exercises and Movements:

Floor Movements

- Return to lying on the back, arms resting by the sides and legs straight.
- Bend one arm back at the elbow. Stretch it, pause, then take it back behind the head (similar to a backstroke movement in swimming), pause.
- Bend it back to the half-way point, and then return to starting position. Repeat with the other arm and continue the sequence.

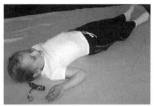

Suggested Exercises and Movements:

Floor Movements

- Lie on back, knees bent, feet flat on the floor and arms resting at the sides.
- Lift head only up as if to hold an orange under the chin.
- Pause.
- Return head to resting position on the floor.
- Repeat the movements several times.

8. Christopher the Caterpillar

Christopher the Caterpillar was getting crosser and crosser. How could his favourite leaf have a water leak?

The more he tried to move, the more he got stuck.

He tried to lift his head and his tail, but his middle (tummy) was stuck in the mud. Up and down he went, but the more he tried to move, the more stuck he got.

Meanwhile…

Inside the pond…

Suggested Exercises and Movements:

Floor Movements

- Return to lying on the tummy.
- Raise head, arms, upper trunk and legs below the knees off the ground. Pause for a few seconds, then return to starting position.
- Repeat the movement, then 'rock' (pivot) forwards and backwards on the tummy in the raised position.

9. Felicity the Fish

Felicity the Fish was getting
ready for her breakfast swim.
Lazily she flipped her tail to one
side, paused for a moment as she
thought about what she was going
to find for breakfast, and then she flipped
to the other side. Like Christopher the Caterpillar,
she was in no hurry to get up.

She slow… ly flipped her tail a few more times, lifted her head and
viewed the pond for the best breakfast spot.

Suggested Exercises and Movements:

Floor Movements

- Lie on the tummy, forehead resting on the floor.
- Lift left hip and let left leg bend slightly below the knee.

- Pause.
- Return to start position.
- Lift right hip and let right leg bend slightly below the knee.
- Repeat movement from side to side.

- Lift head and chest off the ground supporting weight on the forearms (elbows on the ground).
- Repeat bending of lower body on either side.

10. Lizzie the Lizard

Lizzie the Lizard was lying under a rock at the edge of the pond. Something had caught her eye by the garden wall and she wanted to catch it before it ran away. Normally she was a fast mover, but she knew if she went too quickly she would scare it away.

So,

Very slow… ly, she started to bend her head, arm and leg on one side.

She stopped to make sure that the 'thing' had not moved away, and she turned her head and bent her arm and leg on the other side. The 'thing' was still there.

'Ah ha', she thought, 'it hasn't noticed me. Let's see what happens if I move again.' Slow… ly she moved.

Suggested Exercises and Movements:

Floor Movements

- Lie on the tummy, forehead resting on the ground, arms by the sides.
- Turn the head to one side (right) and bend the arm and leg on the same side.
- Pause.
- Turn the head to the opposite (left) side. Straighten the arm and leg on the first (right) side and bend the left arm and leg. Repeat movement slowly from side to side.

11. Bertie the Beetle

Bertie the Beetle had climbed out
of the pond, but his balance was
very poor this morning. He had slipped
in the mud and rolled over on to his
back again.

He lay on his back and slow... ly
turned his head to one side, bending his
arm and leg on the same side at the same
time. In the past he had found this was the best way
of getting back on to his tummy, but this time it did not seem to be working.

He kept trying. When he found it did not work, he tried bending the arm
and leg on the other side.

Suggested Exercises and Movements:

Floor Movements

- Lie on the back with arms and legs straight.
- Turn the head to the right and bend the right arm and leg (keeping them on the floor).
- Return head, arm and leg to the centre.
- Turn the head to the left and bend the left arm and leg. Repeat the sequence several times.

12. Tommy the Tadpole

Tommy the Tadpole had woken up to find that something very strange had happened to him in the night. A few days ago, he had woken up to find that his tail had turned into legs, which had had a very odd effect on his swimming.

This morning he had somehow grown a pair of arms and he did not know what to do with them.

He splashed to the edge of the pond and lay in the mud, resting on his new arms. He turned his head to look over his shoulder and found his arm and leg on the same side turned (bent) in the same direction.

'Strange', he thought, 'it is not at all like I thought it would be out of the water. What a BIG world it is.'

He rested on his new arms again for a moment and then turned his head the other way (also bending the arm and leg to the new viewing side).

After he had done this a few times, to his surprise the world turned around and he found he was the other way up.

'How did I do that?', he said.

He turned his head and rolled back on to his tummy again.

He tried the same thing to the other side and found the world turned around again.

'How clever', he thought, 'perhaps the world out of the water is not so bad after all.'

Suggested Exercises and Movements:

Floor Movements

- Lie on the tummy, resting on the forearms, head up high.
- Turn the head to the right (as if looking over the shoulder), bend the right leg on the ground, lift the right arm off the ground and bend the elbow towards the waist, whilst supporting the upper body on the left arm.

- Pause.
- Return to starting position.

Floor Movements

- Repeat movement to both sides several times.
- Continue movement further until body starts to turn over. Child should arrive in a sitting position.
- Return to start position.
- Repeat movement in the other direction.

13. Bertie the Beetle

Bertie the Beetle made one last
attempt to get himself the right
way up. This time he used
just a little too much 'oomph'.
Instead of rolling and stopping,
he found himself rolling over and
over and over. When he did eventually
stop, the only way to get back to where
he wanted to be was to roll back again.

His head felt quite dizzy and his legs were all wobbly. One long roll in
either direction was more than enough for one day. 'Beetles', he thought, 'were
definitely not designed to roll.'

14. Ali the Aligator

Ali the Aligator la… zily
lifted his head in the early
morning sun. Out of the
corner of his eye he could see
some very attractive insects playing under the trees.

Slow… ly he started to creep towards them.

Suggested Exercises and Movements:
Floor Movements

- Lie on the back. Make sure there is plenty of space.
- Bend the right leg and move it across the body, following the movement through with the right arm until the body starts to roll over.
- Allow the movement to continue, gathering momentum. Stop.
- Return to the centre, head in the middle, arms and legs straight.
- Roll back in the other direction.

Do not over-stimulate your child with this exercise. Child should not carry out more than three rolls in either direction at one time.

Suggested Exercises and Movements:
Floor Movements

- Lie on the tummy.
- Making sure the tummy stays in contact with the floor, crawl forwards, leading with one arm and pushing with the opposite leg, i.e. right arm, left leg; left arm, right leg once.

15. Catharina the Cat

Catharina the Cat was asleep at the bottom of the garden which ran down to the pond. She rai… sed her head and rested on her front paws to look at the day.

'Time for a morning stalk', she thought.

She pushed with her back legs a little and sat up to get a better view. She stre… tched her back by rocking forwards and backwards on her four paws.

Now, she was ready to start looking for some mice.

Slow… ly, so as not to alert any of her prey, she crept through the grass, softly stepping on the early morning dew.

Suggested Exercises and Movements:

Floor Movements

- Lie on the tummy.
- Lift the head and upper body off the ground until resting on the forearms.
- Push the bottom up, straighten the arms and lean back until sitting on the ankles (like a sitting cat).
- Gently rock forwards and backwards from this position.
- Creep forwards on hands and knees as if 'stalking' prey.

16. Beatrice the Butterfly

Beatrice the Butterfly just loved the sun. She was never happier than when she could dance from flower to flower, feeling the warmth of the sun on her wings.

17. Standing Statue

In the middle of the garden was Standing Statue. He never seemed to mind the weather or grow tired. Day and night, winter, spring, summer and autumn, he stood still, guarding the water lilies on the pond.

18. Stiff as a Soldier

Someone had been playing in the garden and left a toy soldier behind. The soldier was a guard who normally stood in his sentry box outside Buckingham Palace. Like Standing Statue, the soldier stood quite, quite still, waiting for his comrade to relieve him of his duty.

Suggested Exercises and Movements:
- Standing with arms outstretched.
- Gently wave the arms like wings.
- Move around the room from object to object, stopping at each object as if to smell a flower.

Suggested Exercises and Movements:
- Stand with feet apart as if in the military 'at ease' position.
- Close the eyes and stand still for several seconds. (Stand behind your child in case he/she loses their balance.)
- Open the eyes and repeat.

Suggested Exercises and Movements:
- Stand with feet together, arms by the sides.
- Stand in the military position of 'attention' for several seconds with the eyes open.
- Repeat with the eyes closed.

(Stand behind your child in case he/she loses their balance.)

19. Wilfred the Windmill

In the field beyond the garden stood Wilfred the Windmill. Sometimes he just looked like an odd-shaped house with extra arms.

But when the wind started to blow, he came alive. His arms started to move, slowly at first, turning round and round, whispering in the wind. If the trees started to move more, Wilfred would move with them and his voice would get louder, turning from a whisper to a hum and then 'whoosh, whoosh, whoosh'.

20. Beatrice the Butterfly

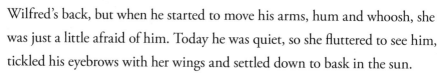

Beatrice fluttered across the field towards Wilfred. Beatrice was known for being a little flighty and rather nervous. There was nothing she loved more than to sunbathe on Wilfred's back, but when he started to move his arms, hum and whoosh, she was just a little afraid of him. Today he was quiet, so she fluttered to see him, tickled his eyebrows with her wings and settled down to bask in the sun.

It was going to be a good day.

Suggested Exercises and Movements:
- Stand with feet together.
- Arms crossed diagonally in front of the body (like the sails of a windmill).
- Slowly rotate the arms outwards (in opposite directions) making circular movements. Arms should move across each other when they return to the centre.

Suggested Exercises and Movements:
- Stand with arms outstretched.
- Gently wave the arms up and down, and run around in an empty space.
- Stop as if 'resting' for a moment.
- Run around again.

Additional activities

- Marching to the music of a military band
- Hopping
- Skipping

Groups

- Ring a ring a roses
- Oranges and lemons
- Traditional country dancing

[1] Levinson, H N, 1994. *Smart but feeling dumb*. New York. Warner Books.

[2] Harrison M, Stuart Clark C, (Eds.), 2004. *A poem for everyone. All kinds of poems about all kinds of people*. Oxford. Oxford University Press.

Chapter 6

A Day in the Garden
A Story for Parents and Children, with Suggested Activities

The following story can be used in several ways:

1. As a bedtime story for children and parents to enjoy together, or in nursery or reception classes, or as part of group 'rhyme time' sessions.
2. A play activity for parents or carer and child. The parent reads the story and as the child becomes familiar with the characters in the story, the child acts out the part of the characters.
3. A more structured daily activity for children from about three years of age, where there may be minor concerns about a child's development of balance or coordination. The suggested exercises may be carried out every day for a period of up to six months.

Please note that if you have any concerns about your child's physical development, please check with your health visitor before carrying out any daily programme of exercises.

If your child is currently receiving treatment for a related disorder, check with your consulting physician or therapist before using any of the suggested exercises.

A New Day

All was quiet in the garden. Night had covered the flowers and creatures in a cloak of darkness. The flowers had curled up inside their petals to keep warm, and most of the creatures except Bertie the Badger and Mol the Owl (who both worked at night) were sound asleep.

As a chink of light started to rise in the distant sky, the birds began to chatter.

'Time to get up; time to get up; it's a beautiful day; the worms are out and it's time to play.'

'No time to sleep; can't stay still; too much to do; time to eat; come along, fly… with me; come and greet the dawn; it's a beau… tiful day.'

As the birds swooped and sang at the joy of greeting a new day, the other inhabitants of the garden began to stir.

Dizzy the Daisy was a sun lover. Night time was all right because she could wrap her petals around herself into a warm blanket, disappear inside the covers and dream of following the sun in its path all day long. But when night started to slip away, she longed to see the sun again

Morning exercises

Lie on the back with arms crossed, hands curled, resting on shoulders, knees bent and ankles crossed, curled up.

and did not like to wake up to a grey or dreary day.

As the light started to tickle her petals, she gingerly opened just one of them to feel if it was warm enough to come out. A drop of dew had collected on her leaf and she shivered to try to make it roll off. 'Atishoo…', she sneezed, as the cold morning air got up her nose, 'atishoo…' This time the dewdrop did fall to the ground and she started to feel a little warmer.

Dizzy was very vain. She knew she was pretty, but could never quite believe that other flowers in the garden were not more noticeable than her. This meant that she always tried to be the first at everything, in the hope that she would be noticed. This included making sure she was the first flower to flash her petals in the mornings.

Dizzy's need to be noticed may have been because she was in fact quite small and one of a family of many daisies on the lawn. Not that there was anything wrong with being a daisy, it was just that some of the bigger flowers such as Lupin and Dahlia seemed to attract more attention, much more admiration from passing bees, and showed off so.

Slowly, she opened out her petals

Slowly uncurl the fingers and toes. Pause.

Curl the fingers and toes. Pause.

Slowly open out first the fingers and toes.
Uncross the arms and legs and slowly open them out.
(Do not straighten the arms and legs completely.)

one by one and **Dizzy** reasoned that being one very small flower amongst many others meant the only way to be noticed was to look her best at all times. She stre… tched out her petals (head and neck), turning to one side and then the other, as she tried to decide which way flattered her most. She fluttered her petals at Mr Sun, beaming down at her from a small corner of the garden. Still not satisfied, she thought, if only I was a little taller, not only could I get nearer to the sun but I would have a better view of the comings and goings in the garden.

Making an enormous effort, she pu… shed her roots (toes) down as far as she could under the ground and sprea… d her leaves (hands) as far out as they would go. This was hard work and she could only stretch herself this far for one to two seconds.

' Whoooooo…', she said, 'this morning work-out is really tiring.'

She rested for a few moments before trying again. After the fifth time she stopped, feeling quite exhausted.

'Dear me', she thought, 'Dizzy, you really are very unfit.'

By this time her roots and leaves were beginning to ache so much that she curled and squeezed them a few

Slowly stretch the neck back (without straining).

Gently wave hands and feet as if wafting them in the air.

Stop waving hands and feet. Stretch arms and hands, legs and feet as far as is comfortable.

Relax.

Curl and uncurl hands and feet a few times.

times, finally giving them a good shake before rearranging her petals so that they were in the best aspect to face the sun.

Shake hands and feet a few times.

'Dizzy my dear', said **Mr Sun**, 'there really is no need to go to so much trouble. Provided there are no clouds in the sky, I would shine on you in the morning anyway. The only time I can't see you is when the garden wall gets in the way as I move across the garden during the day. You are quite lovely, my dear, and there really is no need to make so much effort for me.'

Rest.

Dizzy felt her petals turn a deeper shade of pink at the edges as she blushed. Mr Sun had not only noticed her, he had talked to her as well. Everyone knew that Mr Sun was the King of the Garden, and it was he who decided whether it was warm or cold, night or day, how much you grew and whether you had a good breakfast or not. For a few moments, she was so overcome, she quite forgot to worry about how she looked and stood with her mouth open in surprise.

Dizzy also knew that if you made Mr Sun cross he could make life very uncomfortable. Only once had she seen him angry. For a whole day he had blazed down on the garden, not allowing a cloud in the sky to pass in front of him.

She and the other flowers had got hotter and hotter, more and more thirsty, and she had been so tired by the middle of the afternoon that she had not been able to keep her petals open until bedtime, letting them droop limply as she stood exhausted, longing for him to pass through the garden so she could rest in the shade of the garden wall. She did not know what had made him so fierce that day, but she was clever enough to know that while it was wonderful to be noticed, she never wanted to do anything to make him angry again.

The birds had gone past their first burst of excitement at the new day. Having swooped down to pick up grubs and the first worms of the morning for breakfast, they were now content to fly gently from bush to bush, hopping from leaf to leaf and gossiping amongst themselves.

Meanwhile, **Christopher the Caterpillar** was asleep up under a pile of leaves. Unlike the birds, who seemed to have boundless energy from the moment daylight appeared, Christopher was not a morning person. It took him a

Daytime exercises

Lie on the tummy.

long time to wake up, and he found the
noise of the birds very tiresome.

He stre… tched a little, and then
quickly curled up into a ball again.

*Curl up into a ball and then
stretch out.
Repeat two or three times.*

'Too soon', he thought, 'just another
few minutes' sleep. If only those birds
would be quiet.'

Just as he was settling into a lovely
dream all about cabbage leaves and how
good they tasted, something started to
disturb his bed of leaves. Not only was
it disturbing his bed, it was actually
walking all over it.

His first reaction was to curl up
tighter into a ball in the hope that
the uninvited guest would leave, but
the visitor appeared to be making
itself quite at home, scrabbling and
burrowing at his bed.

Curl up again.

'Bother', he thought. 'I suppose I
shall have to get up.'

'Has that dreadful din quietened
down yet?'

'If it wasn't for those noisy flying
things I would be able to sleep until
noon every day. As it is, I have to get up
long before I am ready, and I don't
like it. What is it about this
garden that some people
get up when they feel like
it, with no thought for anyone
else? It really is most inconsiderate.'

This time, he lifted his head and neck up to try to nudge his way through the bed of leaves and dislodge the unwanted visitor.

For a moment the visitor stopped scrabbling and stood perfectly still. When Christopher became still, the visitor started moving again.

'Would you mind?', said Christopher. 'It really is very rude to walk all over someone's bed when they are still sleeping in it.'

The visitor scuttled round in small circles, stirring the leaves into an untidy pile, right on the top of Christopher's head. Soon the bedding and visitor felt so heavy that he had to lower his head to the ground again.

'I say, this really is terribly rude. Would you please get off?', he mumbled with his face on the ground.

'So sorry, so sorry. Oh dear. Oh dear, oh dear. How silly of me. Of course I will get off at once.'

The visitor was **Wenna the Wood Louse**, who was very well intentioned but had the most dreadfully poor eyesight, and was always bumping into things and getting in the way. This morning she had mistaken a pile of leaves with Christopher underneath it for a pile of twigs, and had been trying to find her way with her feet.

Lie on the tummy with legs straight, arms resting by the sides, head in the centre, resting on the forearms.

Slowly tip the head up a little way until the back of the head is in line with the body.

Pause.

Slowly lower the head to the ground so that the forehead is resting on the floor again.

Rest.

Go up on to hands and knees.

The more anxious she became, the faster she moved and the more flustered she got, losing any sense of direction and turning around in small circles.

'For goodness sake, woman, stop fussing and think', said Christopher.

'Oh yes, oh yes, of course, how sensible of you. All I have to do is stand still and I will be able to work out which way to go next.'

'Just don't stand there for too long. You are giving me a headache.'

'I won't be a moment, but I feel so giddy and I can't think which way to go.'

She started to turn around the other way, in the hope that she could undo her giddiness, but this was too much for Christopher.

'If you don't get off my bed this instant, I am going to arch my back and tip you off', he said.

Turn round twice in one direction.
Pause.
Close the eyes and stay still for five seconds.
Open the eyes.

Turn round twice in the other direction.
Pause.
Staying on hands and knees, close the eyes and stay still for five seconds.
Open the eyes.

Turn round once in each direction again, pausing after each turn for five seconds with the eyes closed.

Wenna was so alarmed that she stopped turning immediately and stood perfectly still, clinging to the remaining leaves with her toes. She knew from experience that if she was tipped on to her back she would get stuck like that, and it might take her all day to roll over again.

Christopher bent his head down and arched his back.

Wenna, who was clutching precariously on the falling pile of leaves with her toes, was frozen to the spot.

Christopher lifted his head and hollowed his back.

Wenna started to lose her grip.

Christopher arched and hollowed his back again.

'Oooooh', cried Wenna, as she slowly tumbled off the pile of leaves, rolled over to land on a soft mound of earth, and ended up lying on her back with her legs in the air.

'Oh, this is so undignified', she said.

She turned her head from side to side to see if she could figure out the best way to roll over, but each time she turned her head, her arms and legs straightened on the same side, stopping her from rolling over.

Wenna brought her head back to the middle and clapped her hands in

Lying on the tummy, slowly flex the neck and arch the back.

Slowly extend the neck and hollow the back.

Repeat the movements a little faster.

Stop the movements and slowly roll over several times (as if rolling off a pile of pillows) until lying on the back.

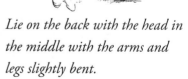

Lie on the back with the head in the middle with the arms and legs slightly bent.

Slowly turn the head from side to side, straightening the arm and leg on the side to which the head is turned, but keeping the opposite arm and leg bent.

agitation, trying to make her very little brain work harder to solve the problem.

'There must be a way', she thought. She remembered that when she became anxious and flustered she could never think properly, so she lay calmly for a few moments, gazing at the canopy of trees beneath the sky as she tried to work out what to do next.

Next time, when she turned her head to one side, she stretched her fingers and tried to reach for a twig.

'If only I can grip the twig with my fingers, I can pull myself over', she thought; but however hard she tried, the twig remained just out of her reach. She tried to the other side but the twigs were even further away.

She remembered that her father always used to tell her that her problem was she tried to do everything too quickly, and if only she slowed down she would not be so clumsy.

Next time she turned her head as slowly as she could, and instead of reaching for the twig, she tucked her arm to the side of her body and brought the other arm and leg across. This time she started to feel herself turning.

'Not quite far enough', she thought, but no amount of pushing would make her roll any further.

Return the head to the middle and make small repeated clapping movements with the hands.

Lie still for a few seconds with the head in the middle, feet on the floor, knees bent and arms flexed ('resting' position).

Turn the head to one side, stretching the arm, fingers and leg on the same side only.

Turn the head to the other side, stretching the arm, fingers and leg on the same side.
Repeat 2 or 3 times.
Return the head to the middle, feet on the floor, knees bent and arms flexed (resting position).

Slowly turn the head to one side, but this time keep the arm and leg on the same side flexed and tucked in to the body. Bend the arm and leg on the opposite side and bring them across the body to the midline of the body.

Return head, arms and legs to 'resting' position.
Repeat the movements to the other side.

She tried the same thing to the other side, but still could not turn quite far enough.

She returned to the middle and then started to rock from side to side. Each time she moved to one side a little further, until finally as she rocked to one side, arms and leg tucked in, she brought the other arm and leg across and her world started to move. For one moment everything was upside down; the next, she was back on her hands and feet again.

Gently rock from side to side. Repeat movements above from side to side, rocking gently until the body starts to roll over.

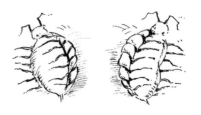

To her horror, she found herself face to face with Christopher; and unable to bear any further scolding from him, she scuttled off into the undergrowth.

Christopher was ready for breakfast and after all his early morning exercise had worked up quite an appetite. Normally he would have made his breakfast from local leaves, but feeling in need of something more substantial he started to work his way towards his favourite milkweed plant on the other side of the lawn.

Lie on the tummy.

He lifted his head, stretched his neck, shrugged his shoulders and started to amble along the caterpillar trail by arching and hollowing his back and pushing with his feet. It took a long time and a lot of effort to go only a short way, but as he slithered on to the damp grass it was easier

Lift up the head.
Shrug and unshrug the shoulders.
Arch and hollow the back a few times.
Bed the toes into the ground and push off with the toes.

to glide along the surface. Mr Sun was shining down, and by the time he reached the edge of the grass he was not only hungry and thirsty but also hot and tired.

He wriggled on to a patch of earth next to his favourite plant Miss Milkweed, and for a few moments rested under the shade of her leaf. All he had to do now was climb up on to the leaf, and breakfast would be his.

This was easier said than done. First he had to lift up his head, neck and shoulders, using his arms to support his weight. Then, gripping the stalk with his fingers he had to pull himself up on to the stalk. Using a combination of pulling with his hands and walking with his feet, he climbed up the stem until he was resting on the leaf.

Once there he started to munch.

It had taken him so long to get up, to reach Miss Milkweed and climb up on to her leaf, that it was now nearly lunchtime. He ate more than he had intended and started to feel quite sleepy.

'I had better not fall asleep here', he thought. ' I might fall off, or worse still get sun burned.'

It was nearing the middle of the day and Mr Sun was doing a splendid job of keeping the garden warm. He turned round so that he could go down feet first,

Using a combination of these movements, slowly move forwards.

(This is much easier if done on a slippery surface such as a wood-laminated floor.)

After a small distance. Stop.

Find a sturdy flat surface with which to make a short slide. Slowly climb up the surface.

Slowly slide back down the surface, feet first.

slithering down Miss Milkweed's stalk. This was much easier and more fun than climbing up, and he would have liked to have done it again.

Slowly he crawled back through the grass until he reached some shade. Hot and tired after his exercise, he shed some of his outer clothes and used them to form a hammock, which he hung between two stems of a plant. Wearily he crawled in, lay on his back, and as he gently swayed from side to side he watched the patterns made by the light and shade on the under-side of the leaf until his eyes became heavier and heavier. He hummed gently to himself… and soon he fell into a deep sleep. He no longer heard the comings and goings in the garden. He did not see Mr Sun pass through the garden or Queen Moon rise in the evening. He did not feel the rain fall on the leaves or see the grass growing around him. He slept and he slept and he slept.

In his sleep he travelled. He was able to see all of the garden as if he was standing high above it; his legs no longer felt tired and he dreamt that he had grown big beautiful arms painted the colour of some of the brightest flowers in the garden, and he felt as light as air. For the first time, as

Squat with arms to the sides.
Gently flap arms up and down.

he started to wake up he did not feel cross or tired. He felt as if today was going to bring something new and special, as if something magical was going to happen.

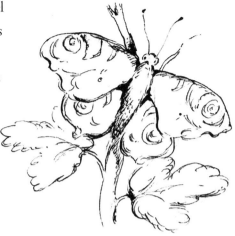

He opened his eyes and found that he was covered in morning dew. He shivered and shook himself. To his surprise he started to lift up into the air. He shook himself again and tried to stretch, expecting his head and body to feel heavy. As he stretched, two large and two smaller beautiful wings unfurled from where his legs used to be. Shaking off the last of the morning dew, he spread his wings and flew out into the sunlight. Below him he could see Dizzy preening herself in preparation for a new day. For a moment he flew between her and Mr Sun casting a shadow.

'Oh Mr Sun, please don't go away so soon', she said, as she started to uncurl her petals to greet another new day.

Spread the arms, slowly stand up and run around, slowly flapping arms up and down.
Pause as if resting on leaf for five seconds.
Run again.
Pause.
Repeat a few times.

Examples of two of the songs from *Wings of Childhood* can be found below. You will see that 'The Caterpillar' and 'The Butterfly' provide a natural musical sequel to the story above.

In a nutshell:

- Children's movement development mirrors stages of evolution.
- See photographs in Chapter One for the sequence of movement development in the first year of life.
- Practice of these movements helps to integrate centres involved in movement control and posture. This can be done through games, stories, songs and activities.

Chapter 7

Are You Steady? Are You Ready?

The concept that physical development lays the foundations for mental functioning is not new. Jean Piaget (1896–1980), a biologist who later carried out research in psychology specialising in how children learn, recognised that children and adults think and learn in different ways and that development strongly influences how children progress in both.

Piaget concluded that there were four key stages in the cognitive development of children. The first stage he described as the **sensory-motor stage**, covering the stage from birth to approximately two years of age. He described this time as being centred on 'schemas'. A schema is a mental concept that informs a person about what to expect from a variety of experiences and situations. Schemas develop based on information provided by life experiences and are then stored in memory. Piaget deduced that the first schemas an infant forms concern movement. As we have seen in previous chapters, much of a baby's behaviour is initially reflexive in nature, triggered by certain stimuli, but within only a few weeks of birth the baby begins to 'make sense' of sensory information, and learns to use its muscles and limbs for purposeful movement. These developments are known as 'action schemas'. During the sensory-motor stage, information is acquired about the self in relation to the world, time, space and the rudiments of cause and effect.

According to Piaget, babies are unable to consider anyone else's wants or interests and are therefore considered to be egocentric (self-centred).

The second developmental stage, Piaget described as the **pre-operations stage**, normally spanning from two to seven years of age. During this stage thought processes develop alongside an extending vocabulary with which to describe them. Several 'levels' of thinking are also typical of this stage, including 'animism', in which a child believes that everything else in the world has feeling and consciousness; 'symbolism' – when something stands for or symbolises something else; and 'moral realism' – a belief that the child's way of seeing right and wrong is universal. Because at this stage of development a child can only see one aspect of a situation at a time, they cannot see others' point of view resulting in an inflexible approach to rules. All of these ways of thinking are consistent with underlying egocentricity, although gradually over this stage children do start to recognise that they are not the sole centre of the universe and allow others to be the focus of attention.

The **concrete operational stage** (seven to 11/12 years) sees thought processes becoming more rational, mature and 'adult like', or more 'operational', and continues well into the teenage years. The process was divided by Piaget into two stages, the **concrete operations**, and the **formal operations stage**, the latter developing through adolescence (11–16 years).

During the concrete operational stage, the child has the ability to develop logical thought about an object, provided the object is present and they are able to manipulate it. During the concrete operational stage children start to understand that the essence of something remains constant even if elements of it appear to change; for example, a pile of blocks or the same blocks scattered over the floor contain the same number, irrespective of their arrangement.

As the fourth, **formal operations stage** develops, the ability to manipulate thoughts and ideas in the absence of an object improves, bringing with it the capacity for abstraction. This enables adolescents to reason beyond a world of concrete reality to a world of possibilities, and to operate logically on symbols and information that do not necessarily refer to objects and events in the real world (abstract thinking).

An example of the transition from concrete operational to formal operational thinking can be seen in the ability to understand and manipulate symbols in maths. When my daughter was 11 she struggled to understand the concept of fractions, decimals and percentages, as they were being taught at school as abstract concepts. She had decided that she hated maths and couldn't do it. A maths tutor took her back to an earlier stage of developmental thinking. He asked her to line up 100 toy Roman soldiers in rows of 10. He then asked her why they were called centurions, and what other words she could think of starting with the prefix 'cent'? She came up with 'centipede', 'century' and 'centimetre'.

'Why?', he asked, did she think all these words began with 'cent'. What did they have in common?

It took her a few seconds to come up with, 'a centipede has 100 legs; a century describes a period of 100 years, and I don't know why a centimetre is a centimetre.'

'Well', he said, 'the common denominator in all of these words is that they describe something involving the number 100.'

A light began to dawn.

'Now', he said, 'I would like you to count all of the soldiers you have lined up. How many are there?'

'100.'

'So, why do you think the soldiers are called centurions?'

'Because each soldier is one man in a group of one hundred men.'

'So, if you were going to write that in numbers instead of describing it with words, how would you write it?'

'1/100.'

'Now, I want you to divide them into two groups, with exactly the same number in each group. How many are there in each group?'

'Fifty.'

'And how many groups are there?'

'Two.'

'So if you were to put one group on one side, how would you describe that group?'

'One out of two.'

'And if you were to write that using numbers instead of words, how would you write it?'

'½.'

'Which in words is, what?'

'Half.'

'And if you were to describe that as 50/100, recognising that per cent means a smaller number out of one hundred?'

'Fifty per cent or 50% – easy!'

'And if you were to write that as a decimal?'

'I don't understand decimals.'

'Well, if I was to write .5 and say .5 is a different way of writing 50/100, 50% or ½, does it start to make sense?'

'It is beginning to.'

'So, why is a centimetre called a centimetre?'

'Because there are one hundred centimetres in a metre.'

So the conversation went on, counting up different groups of soldiers, putting groups aside, and then describing them in words, fractions, percentages and decimals in relation to each other. At the next session, they started to work simply using symbols, but with the soldiers lined up in front of her if she needed them. By the third session she was able to start manipulating fractions and decimals without needing the 'concrete' examples of the soldiers.

In short, teaching of fractions, decimals and percentages at school had started at a too high a level for her developmental level of understanding at the time. Unable to grasp the meaning or permanence of what the symbols represented, the 'language' of maths was incomprehensible. As she could not understand, she assumed she was stupid, hated maths and gave up. By taking her back one stage and providing concrete examples of what words and numbers represented, she was quickly able to succeed.

Another example of the transfer from real objects to abstract thinking was shown in a TV series exploring cultures throughout the world. The presenter joined a group of Chinese six year olds in a maths class. The teacher called out quite difficult sums to them to calculate and the presenter was amazed that the children were able to come up with a correct answer in their heads in matter of seconds. In contrast, he was trying to work out the answer using pencil and paper or a calculator and could not keep up with them. In some dismay, he tapped one of the boys on the shoulder to ask how he worked it out so quickly. 'Easy', was the reply, 'I learned to count using an abacus and now when I am asked an arithmetical problem I 'see' the abacus inside my head, and I know the answer.'

There are two major characteristics of formal operational thought.

The first is 'hypothetico-deductive reasoning'. When faced with a problem, adolescents come up with a general theory of all possible factors that might affect the outcome and deduce from it specific possibilities (hypotheses) that might occur. They then systematically test these possibilities to see which ones do in fact occur in the real world.

The second important characteristic of this stage is that it is 'propositional' in nature. Adolescents can focus on verbal assertions and evaluate their logical validity without having to refer to real life (concrete) circumstances. In contrast, concrete operational children can only evaluate the logic of statements by considering them against concrete evidence.

Piaget's theoretical construct for understanding the progression in children's styles of reasoning over the course of development had a considerable influence on educational thinking in the 1960s, but as with so many developments, as time has passed policy has moved on and has tended to become so focused on educational *end* product results that it has contracted amnesia for the importance of natural developmental stages along the way, in effect, throwing the baby out with the dirty bath water.

Other examples of educational philosophies which have recognised the fundamental role of physical development and experience in learning include those of Maria Montessori, Rudolf Steiner and Donald Hebb.

Maria Montessori was an Italian physician and educator who arrived at an educational approach based on her extensive research and observational work with disabled, non-disabled and 'special needs' children. Montessori noticed that children's spontaneous activity in environments prepared to meet their needs followed an internal pattern of development. She came to regard the role of the educator as being to remove obstacles to this natural development and provide opportunities for it to advance and flourish. Montessori education is characterised by an emphasis on independence, freedom within limits, and respect for a child's natural psychological, physical and social development. Together with her son Mario Montessori she recognised that there are innate, universal human tendencies which were categorised in four periods of human development:

1. Birth to six years
2. Six to 12 years
3. 12 to 18 years
4. 18 to 24 years

Like Piaget, she observed that each stage was characterised by different learning modes strongly guided by the developmental imperatives active at the each period or 'plane' of development. She advocated that educational approaches should be specific to each period. Key features of Montessori education include: Educators setting up special environments to meet the needs of children in three age groups – two and a half years, two and a half to six years, and six and a half to twelve years. Children are encouraged to learn through activities that involve exploration, manipulations, order, repetition, abstraction and communication. Children are guided to use their senses to explore and manipulate materials, and only in the last age group are they steered to deal with abstract concepts based on emerging powers of reasoning, imagination and creativity. In other words, her developmental approach to education starts with the physical leading into the ability to visualise, analyse and mentally manipulate concepts.

Rudolf Steiner (1861–1925) was an academic born in Austria whose ideas founded the basis of Anthroposophy. The priority in the practice of Steiner's philosophy is to provide an unhurried and creative learning environment where children find joy in learning and experience the richness of childhood rather than early specialisation or academic hot-housing. The curriculum follows pedagogical guidelines which give equal attention to the physical, emotional, intellectual, cultural and spiritual needs of each child as an individual, and which work alongside the difference phases of child development. Formal instruction in literacy does not begin until six years of age but much preparation work is done in getting the child *ready* for reading, writing etc. Children are also introduced to other spoken languages (German) in the early years, through songs and actions which mimic the meaning of the words. For example, English children in a Steiner school might have a 'lesson' in a pretty classroom decorated like a room in a Bavarian home. There, they might sing songs about laundry day, matching actions of scrubbing, hanging clothes on a line, ironing etc. to the words of the songs. In this way, children absorb the vocabulary of an additional language in much the same way that children learn their first language, through intonation (music), words describing 'actions' (verbs) and 'naming' (nouns) first.

One of the reasons for introducing a second language as part of education from an early age is that fundamental *differences* between languages such as the precise meaning of words (exact translation is not always possible), phrasing and structure of sentences can enrich understanding and use of our own language. I was struck by one incidence of this when providing a course for teachers in Germany a number of years ago. When trying to explain that the programme I had developed should be applied to a whole class of children, and that the children should only move on to the next stage of exercises when all children in the class had mastered the exercises they were doing and practised them correctly for several weeks, one of the German attendees summarised this long sentence with, 'so you are saying that this is the only time when the slowest child will lead the entire class'. Even simple differences such as the French 's'il vous plaît' compared to the English 'please' alters the *tone* of the request – the former asking for something on the basis of whether the other person pleases to deliver, the latter being more of a demand.

Over time, use and misuse, words also undergo subtle changes in meaning. The French expression 'en retard' means late. The word 'retarded' used to be applied to describe someone with mental disabilities. The term then came to be loosely applied by people calling their friends or others without mental disabilities 'retards' as a term of ridicule or abuse, and it is now no longer used for its original purpose. However, its original application was not intended to be offensive but to describe a slower rate of development and/or processing. In this way, a little knowledge of another language from an early age can help to foster a deeper and more precise understanding of language.

In seeking to express ourselves in another language or translate another language into our own, we are forced to search for different ways of phrasing what we want to say, often reaching closer to the etymological roots of words in common use, thereby enriching vocabulary and enhancing understanding. The tradition of teaching of classics in schools did much the same, in addition to improving the understanding of structure and grammatical rules of language. (I found English grammar very boring at school, but loved the logic behind Latin grammar and came to understand the parts of speech in English through Latin.)

The impact of such methods of teaching and learning have been recognised by others and applied to adult education. George Lozanov, a medical doctor from Sofia in Bulgaria who specialised in psychiatry and psychotherapy with a passion for understanding how human beings learn, developed a method he called Suggestopedia. Suggestopedia was based on two principles – suggestion and pedagogy – which were applied to the learning of foreign languages with remarkable results. Suggestion taps into the beliefs that learners hold about what they are capable of accomplishing by extending the scope and depth of what they believe is possible, while pedagogical principles utilise physical experience such as incorporating music, art, role-playing and games into the curriculum as new material is introduced or being learned, to embed new information into the psyche. Lozanov (like Lazarev at a different stage of development) recognised that there are *reserve capacities of the mind*, which can become blocked by trauma or stress. Lozanov saw that a learning environment which supports the mental, physical and spiritual health of the learner helped the student to rediscover their thirst for learning, thereby uncovering previously hidden talents and capacities. Transposed into a different situation, this approach was described by a master of choristers when he said that, 'I believe if you set a boy a task that he does not think he can do, and you provide the training to support it, he will reach to perform above the level expected of him and exceed his own expectations'.[1]

While Lozanov focused on emotional, mental and physical properties of learning, Donald Hebb (1904–1985), a Canadian psychologist who was influential in the area of neuropsychology, sought to understand how the function of neurons contributed to psychological processes such as learning.[2] His research led him to view psychology as *biological* science in which thought is the product of integrated activity in the brain,[3] with cognitive processes being the consequence of connections between neuron assemblies – a perspective which strongly influenced his views on education and learning.

Hebb viewed motivation and learning as related properties based on experience, in which the environment fires a set of neurons called a cell assembly. Cell assemblies are the physical ingredients of thought and ideas. Cell assemblies work together to form 'phase sequences', which describe streams of thought or habitual ways of thinking unique to the individual. Once formed, cell assemblies and phase sequences can be activated by stimulation of the environment. Children learn by building up these cell assemblies and phase sequences fed by an enriched environment with varied opportunities for sensory and motor experiences, which contribute to the development of the neurological pathways necessary for continued learning in adulthood. To prove his theory Hebb and his daughters observed the behaviour of pet rats raised at home and was able to show that rats raised in an enriched environment showed improved maze learning in adulthood.[4]

This research into environmental enrichment contributed to the development of the Head Start Program. Head Start is a programme for preschool children in low-income families, which aims to prepare children for school by providing cognitively stimulating activities for children who might not receive this type of stimulation in the home. In previous chapters we have already seen how important conversation with an involved and sympathetic listener is for developing speech; how the sounds and sights of reading are gleaned from listening to stories being told, and vocabulary is absorbed from context even when children do not know what individual words mean; and how control of movement both supports and articulates a child's understanding of the universe. While many parents from low-income families do provide these opportunities, children from socially impoverished environments are at greater risk of missing out on this range of experiences, starting school at a disadvantage not because they lack fundamental ability, but because they have not had the range of experiences which act as physical and mental building blocks to support higher aspects of learning.

A report carried out by the National Literacy Trust in 2005 based on a joint survey of by the National Literacy Trust and the National Association of Head Teachers revealed that 74 percent of the 121 heads polled felt that young children's speaking and listening skills had deteriorated in the previous five years, especially the ability to speak audibly and be understood.[5] A poll by I CAN – a national charity working for children with speech and language difficulties – found that 89 percent of nursery workers said they were worried about the growth of speech, language and communication difficulties among pre-school children. Although no single cause could be attached to this decline, 92 percent of them attributed it to the lack of time adults and children spend talking together.[6] Other contributory factors postulated include:

• Prolonged use of dummies.
• Long periods spent in buggies on family days out.
• The impact of forward-facing buggies in which an alert infant or toddler faces the disengaged outside world rather than the facial expressions, responses and interactions of the parent or primary carer.
• Increased use of mobile phones by parents and carers.
• Impact of background noise from electronic devices and media.

Why might some of these apparently small changes in early childhood experience have an impact on the development of speech and language? Let's take the issue of forward-facing buggies first.

Suzanne Zeedyk, a former researcher at the University of Dundee, carried out a small study in 2008 to confirm whether or not the direction that a buggy faces has a significant impact on how adults interact with their baby.

> We found that simply turning the buggy around (to face the parent) doubles the amount of conversation that babies experience. The most surprising thing we discovered, once we looked closely at what was happening for children on High Streets in Britain, was just how infrequently babies seemed to be taking part in conversations with parents. Of the nearly 3,000 observations that volunteers made of parent–child pairs, talking was observed in only 22% of those observations. Talking was twice as likely to be happening when children were being carried or walking (more than 40%) than when they were in strollers (less than 20%).[7]

These findings were replicated by a study carried out in New Zealand by Dr Ken Blaiklock at the Unitec Institute of Technology in New Zealand, which showed the same three key patterns in relation to the amount of conversational interaction between parent and child when out in forward-facing buggies. Blaiklock's observations showed that interactions were even lower in New Zealand when the child was facing away from the parent (5 percent to 22 percent in the United Kingdom) and that the model of buggy most commonly used for transport out-stripped parent-facing models by 68 percent to 12 percent.[8]

The forces that drive marketing and child development are not necessarily mutually beneficial. While manufacturers of baby equipment need to sell products and are very slick when it comes promoting the latest designs, many parents, particularly parents with their first child, are simply unaware of the benefits of having baby facing them when out and about. Amongst less-educated parents, there can simply be ignorance about why parent–child conversation is important. This was illustrated by a case a colleague was working with professionally. She had been assessing an older child in the family for signs of neuromotor immaturity. Towards the end of the assessment a friend returned to the office with a younger child who had been taken for a walk around town during her sibling's assessment. My colleague started to chat away to the toddler in the buggy. The mother watched this exchange and after a few moments, with genuine surprise asked, 'Why are you wasting your time talking to her? She's only a baby'.

Such parental attitudes to parent–child verbal interaction are not unusual. When working with a family with a younger child who had reading problems, as the child's neuromotor skills started to improve and the eye movements needed to support fluent reading developed, we were discussing the best time of day for the family to carry out his exercises. Both parents worked and the only practical time available was bedtime. I suggested that the exercises could be done just before the bedtime story. The conversation went something like this.

'We don't read him a bedtime story', said the parents in unison.

'Now, he can follow a line of print, this would be a good thing to introduce every night, so that he can start to match the visual symbols to the sound of your voice.'

'But if we start reading him a story, the other two children will want one.'

'Is that a bad thing?'

'We have never read any of them a bedtime story.'

'Well, it is never too late to start, and it might help the other two at school as well, not just with reading and spelling but also creative writing.'

'We don't know how. No one ever read us a story at bedtime when we were little.'

And so, the gaps from one generation can be passed down to the next, not through lack of will but a lack of childhood experience and awareness of why simple things are important.

As mobile phones have become the norm in technology-driven societies for the majority of the population, particularly the young, parents spend an increasing amount of time either talking on or scanning these devices, socially 'unavailable' to their child while attention is focused on the device.

There is also the issue of living in increasingly noisy environments. In cities it is commonplace to see adults walking to work wearing headphones, cocooned in a bespoke world of their own which shuts out not only the noise of the external environment but also awareness and attention to what is taking place around them. While adults may choose to do this, young children cannot. An experiment carried out investigating the impact of background noise on the ability to hear salient sounds found that the ability to hear and discriminate between different sounds is impaired as levels of background noise increase.[9] One defence mechanism against a noisy environment is to learn to 'shut off' when competing sounds are present. Homes in which a background of radio, TV, phone and computer alerts, in addition to domestic equipment and traffic noise can, in theory, influence a child's desire and ability to listen as well as affecting the ability to sustain attention on one task.

The importance for all children of a high-quality home learning environment where parents are actively engaged in activities with their children encouraging intellectual and social development was highlighted by Professor Kathy Sylva in a report for a House of Commons select committee as being more important than parents' social class and level of education: 'More important than the mother's educational qualities is what the mother does with the child. Education matters… but if the mother reads to the child, plays rhyming games, sings songs, talks about letters and sound and takes the child to the library, these behaviours at home are more important.'[10]

This brings us back to the neurological connections involved in learning observed by Hebb and his belief that not only childhood learning but also adult learning is enhanced by an enriched environment during childhood. This later or 'second type' of learning, which continues through adulthood, is more rapid and insightful because the cell assemblies and phase sequences have already been created and can be rearranged in any number of ways.[11] Not only are neuronal connections strengthened through repetition of actions, but new challenges and practice create new ones. I sometimes liken this to a network of motorways linking in to minor roads all over the land mass – learning both builds and reflects highways of the mind.

So, what does an enriched environment involve? How can parents provide such an environment, without over-stimulating and pushing their children too soon?

Learning confidence begins with physical confidence in space, in feeling safe, accepted and nurtured. In this sense, everything begins with Love.

Love is expressed by parents in the first months of life through caring for their child – through touch, feeding, sensitivity, care and attention to their child's needs – and learning to know when a child is content to be left alone. Nurturing begins with touch and is predominantly sensory in nature for the first six months of life. These are the seeds of non-verbal communication and also, many years later, sexual communication between lovers.

Movement opportunity, first within the safe embrace of the parent's body and later through the expression of free movement, is the primary medium through which the infant vestibular system begins its training. From being held, rocked and carried in a parent's arms, the vestibular system begins to learn to respond to different planes and speeds of motion. This is the very beginning of balance.

Balance is defined in The Oxford Dictionary of Etymology as 'uncertainty, doubt, risk' – a very different interpretation from what is commonly thought of as balance today, more usually taken to mean a state of equilibrium. But the original definition is more correct, because the exercise of balance is a state of constant adjustment in the pursuit of stability. Balance is a continuously *active* state needed to resist the force of gravity, gravity being the one constant force experienced by every living thing. Initially, control of balance involves multiple body parts and large movements, but as control develops, the adjustments involved become more refined, with the highest level of balance being the ability to stay totally still. Walking and running are sequential processes which have evolved to stop us falling over. As control of balance is transferred from one leg in a forward direction, the next leg must be placed, and so on. When control of balance is insecure, it affects more than simply physical stability; it awakens corresponding physical sensations and emotional feelings of uncertainty, doubt and awareness of risk in relation to falling and loss of control. If this continues through childhood into adult life it can predispose a person to suffer from anxiety, avoidant behaviour and, in extreme, the onset of 'secondary' neuroses such as panic disorder and agoraphobic tendencies (Blythe 1975).[12] Blythe termed these anxiety-related conditions, which fail to respond to pharmacological or psychological interventions, as 'secondary neuroses', as it was his belief that they developed as a secondary consequence of underlying immaturity in the functioning of the central nervous system.

Balance develops alongside muscle tone (anti-gravity), posture and use of the body in space. In this sense, movement opportunity and practice are the infant gym. From a mother's arms, an infant graduates to floor time, where free use of the arms, legs, fingers, toes (active proprioceptive feedback) and head control start to develop. During each one of these stages, parents can include elements of earlier ones, using infant massage (passive proprioceptive stimulation), swimming, creating an infant obstacle course from household items, outdoor play, etc.

Posture describes position in space and *attitude* – originally meaning the manner in which the body is held, but also related to *aptitude*. Once again, language recognises a physical basis for what we have come to understand as psychological states or abilities. With control of posture comes increased mastery of the exercise of balance and a stable platform for centres involved in the control of eye movements, which collectively support visual perception. Congruence in information supplied to the brain from the eyes and body enables a child to hold stability within the self and process information from the outside world. The building blocks for postural control are put in place in the first year of life, reaching major milestones in learning to sit, support the body on four points (crawling position), standing and walking; but postural adaptation to changing conditions continues to be practised and integrated for many years to come. At the other end of life, as postural control starts to deteriorate, confidence and independence also start to decline.

Figure 7. 1: Emerging postural control

As parents, allow your child time, space and opportunity to explore his/her body in relation to the world through free play and provide support when needed.

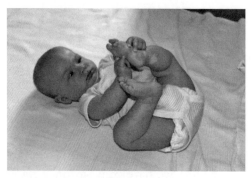

Figure 7.2: 'So this is where I begin and end in space'

Figure 7.3: Free to roam

Postural control contributes to poise. Poise is variously defined as, 'be or cause to be balanced or suspended', 'graceful and elegant bearing in a person' – and describes the ability to sustain stillness between one phase of movement and another. If the highest level of balance is the ability to remain totally still, then poise is the product of well-developed balance and postural control. Such control not only provides a sense of stability and a sound basis for coordination in the person, it also 'speaks' to the outside world, potentially affecting how other people treat us. It has been argued that posture and demeanour may increase vulnerability to victimisation, and that children[13] and adults[14] with unusual posture or gait are more likely to be picked on.

Balance and posture provide the stable framework for **coordination**. Coordination describes the ability to use different parts of the body together smoothly and efficiently and develops over time through use and practice. Skill in coordination can range from basic to exquisite, depending on a combination of hereditary traits and innate ability combined with training and practice. Some families seem to have a natural tendency to develop certain skills earlier or later than others, but the general advice is to provide your child with plenty of opportunity to enjoy the process of learning and refining physical skills at his or her own pace. The watchwords in any learning process are joy and discovery. When there is joy, children are motivated to learn and to continue to persevere at something when they do not at first succeed. This is very different from insisting on a child continuing to try something at which they have become frustrated or afraid.

Play is the work of children. In attempting to define play, definition tends to limit what play is about, because play is free and its scope boundless in as far as it encompasses behaviour which is freely chosen, personally directed and comes from within. It is performed for its own sake, and is an expression of life's natural energy force or joie de vivre. Rough and tumble play is particularly important for young mammals, as the physical contact involved helps to build bonds between group members, tests strengths and boundaries, teaches group members socially how to fit in with the pack, and develops life survival skills through play acting, chasing, fleeing, waiting to pounce, etc. If some mammals do not engage in rough and tumble play when young, they tend to be rejected by the pack as they grow up. As infants become more robust, they usually delight in gentle rough and tumble play when in the right mood and within safe boundaries. Fathers are particularly good at this type of play, which takes children beyond the physical experiences they are able to make by or for themselves, extending their experience and joy in discovery. It also helps to teach self-regulation.

Play does not have to include someone else. Whether it be purely physical, or a few years later, imaginative, time engaged in play is both explorative and creative and involves trial and error. Modern parents often think their child must either be entertained or doing something most of the time, but just as adequate stimulation is important, so also boredom can be the mother of invention as well as mischief! Children, like adults, need time to muse, to absorb what they have seen in their world, to imitate and play act events in real life, to organise and understand. Constant stimulation results in stress, while conversely growth (both physical and mental) often occurs out of sight in the quiet moments when stimulation is reduced. Growth hormone, for example, is secreted at night; seeds planted in the ground germinate in the dark, and ideas often appear when awakening from sleep. Provided a child has access to adequate attention when needed, he or she can amuse themselves for quite long periods of time. This type of play can involve toys (tools for play) or be purely ruminative or imaginative. One of the most engaging periods of imaginative play coincides with the time when 'role play speech', followed by 'private speech', emerges.

I can remember many instances of these stages occurring both from my own childhood and bringing up my children. When my daughter was sent to her room for misbehaving, I would frequently hear her taking her favourite doll out of the toy box, placing it on her bed and hearing her say, 'you have been a *very* naughty dolly'. The monologue could continue for several minutes as her doll was told exactly what she had done wrong. This was role-play speech (addressed to an object), whereas private speech is 'typically defined, in contrast to social speech, as speech addressed to the self (not to others) for the purpose of self-regulation (rather than communication)'.[15] During the period of role-play speech, which coincides with Piaget's stages of 'animism' and 'symbolism', children act out in their play real-life situations exploring the feelings and dynamics involved.

Vygotsky (1987) was the first psychologist to document the importance of private speech, which he considered to be the transition point between social and inner speech, the moment in development where language and thought unite to constitute verbal thinking.[16] In other words, private speech is the earliest manifestation of inner speech, the process through which we problem-solve, reflect upon and translate imaginings into language.

Private speech is when we address ourselves aloud, apparently unconcerned about whether anyone else can hear. 'How could I have done that?' 'What I need to do next is…' It is the external expression of verbal reasoning which children use, most commonly between three and seven years of age, when involved in tasks of intermediate difficulty (those that they are capable of doing but need to work out 'how' during the process). Private speech helps in self-regulation by planning and organising thoughts. Whereas the right hemisphere of the brain is involved in holistic, visual and intuitive processes, the left side is more logical and analytical. If it cannot see an immediate solution to a problem, the left hemisphere will break it down into small pieces and seek to re-assemble them piece by piece. While the right side has more connections in a downward direction to centres involved in feelings and emotions, and matures slightly ahead of the left in the early years, the left brain is logical and uses language to express itself. Private speech recruits the left brain to assist in solving problems that the right brain cannot resolve alone (and vice-versa). This increased cooperation between left and right sides of the brain heralds the beginning of more mature ways of thinking and helps to regulate feelings of confusion and frustration when a task cannot be accomplished immediately.

This stage of 'talking to oneself' eventually becomes internalised, so that not only challenging *tasks* but problems of any kind can be worked through mentally. I know that when I am worried or upset by something I have long 'conversations' inside my head, as I attempt to work out through internal verbal reasoning what if anything can be done and how to accept the situation. Through private speech, children begin to collaborate with themselves – emotional centres discussing with more logical centres how best to solve a problem – this is similar to asking the advice of a more qualified person or starting to develop 'the parent within'.

The 'parent or adult within' describes the ability to apply formerly external regulatory influences to our own behaviour. In other words, children initially rely on the external regulation of the adults around them to guide and modify their behaviour. As they mature, the need for external regulation should gradually be transformed into the ability to regulate the self in response to external stressors, demands and internal needs. Much work has been done on the role of parents acting as external regulators of their child's behaviour and emotional state, suggesting that a combination of sympathetic, responsive, consistent and effective parenting helps children to develop these skills for themselves. Very few parents are perfect, and the nature of parenting is that it is learned on the job and every child is different. What works for one may be counter-productive with another and there is no magic formula. But children who are able to develop the capacity for private speech are demonstrating a first step in beginning to be able to regulate (delay) their own reaction to frustration and modify their response.

Play should continue throughout life, because play is a process through which known things are manipulated, used and remodelled in different ways, and it is through play that creative urges are explored and realised. From the simplest ideas to advance scientific thought, play or experimentation combined with growing knowledge underlie the 'eureka' moment and the materialisation of method from chaos. This is of course an over-simplification – scientific discovery and artistic genius are based on years of knowledge, training and skill – but an important element of invention and creativity is retention of the 'magical thinking' of childhood, which opens a window through which to see and explore known facts in new ways.

The discovery of insulin for the treatment of diabetes provides an example of this. Before the discovery of insulin, diabetes was a feared disease that most certainly led to death. Doctors knew that sugar worsened the condition and that the most effective treatment was to place patients on a reduced sugar diet. At best, this treatment could buy patients a few extra years. In 1889 German physiologist Oskar Minkowski and physician Joseph von Mering, showed that if the pancreas was removed from a dog, the animal developed diabetes. But if the duct through which the pancreatic juices flow to the intestine was tied off so the juices couldn't reach the intestine – the dog developed minor digestive problems but no diabetes. This had been known by doctors for some 30 years before Roger Banting came up with the idea that by tying off the pancreatic ducts in dogs (and later cattle), a secretion could be extracted which might be effective in the treatment of diabetes. This 'idea' was the product of knowledge combined with observation, experimentation and a new way of looking at current knowledge in different way – an adult version of mental play at work.

Artists do something similar when painting a scene. Most of my life, despite studying fine arts for two years at university, I have despaired at my ineptitude at drawing or painting. One day I was lucky enough to observe an art class being given to a group of senior citizens, in which the artist showed them how landscapes could be painted without drawing, simply using colour to build form and perspective. The paintings that materialised were not so much the product of refined hand–eye coordination (although this is a necessary tool in the process), but a product of looking at the world in a different way. I have seen the same artist teach five and six year old children how to paint a landscape in just 15 minutes by asking them to look at what colours they see in the landscape and then put them on to paper. Parents could not believe that their child was capable of producing such a mature work of art. All the artist had done was to enable the child to look at the world with fresh eyes.

Figure 7.4: Looking at the world in new ways

Listening and Vocalising

Listening, babbling and speaking are the seeds of language and literacy. Understanding and use of language is enhanced when children are exposed to using it in a variety of different ways – through conversation, listening to stories, songs, rhymes and poetry – stories and poetry in particular help to extend understanding of the myriad meanings of words and phrases through the exercise of curiosity and imagination.

Learning is most effective when teaching material starts from where the child is, in terms of his/her understanding of the world. In this way, stories and poems which tap into an element of a child's current understanding tend to engage their interest best, particularly if humour and emotion are involved. Peter Dixon, an artist who takes art and poetry into schools ,has written several anthologies for primary school children, that do just this.

Extract from: 'Where Do All the Teachers Go?'
by Peter Dixon[17]

> Where do all the teachers go
> When it's 4 o'clock?
> Do they live in houses
> And do they wash their socks?
>
> Do they wear pyjamas
> And do they watch TV?
> And do they pick their noses
> The same as you and me?
>
> Do they live with other people?
> Have they mums and dads?
> And were they ever children?
> And were they ever bad?
>
> Did they ever, never spell right?
> Did they never make mistakes?
> Were they punished in the corner
> If they pinched the chocolate flakes?
> Etc.

Extract from: 'The Cracked Ceiling'
by Peter Dixon

Do you remember the ceiling
With its candles and carrots and flowers?
How we lay in the bed, not quite sleeping
And told stories for hours and hours?
Do you remember the witch with white fingers,
The King with a crown on his head,
And the monster with plastercrack features
Who scowled and hung over the bed?
We told every stain of that ceiling
We knew every mark from the rain,
And how the great grey anaconda
Swung down from the picture hook rail…

Creative Space and Imagination

I grew up in an old house in which my mother waged a constant battle with décor which never quite reached, or could be maintained, to her high standards. There were always chips in the paintwork, uneven panes of glass in the window and curtains which had become faded by the sunlight over the years. Just like the poem above I can remember seeing animal shapes in the chipped paintwork, exquisite patterns painted by Jack Frost on the inside of the windows in the night (no double glazing or central heating!), swirling patterns in the curtains, and in the summer months, lying on the grass looking up at the trees imagining the canopy was the roof of a house in the forest with the clouds as pictures. I can remember reversing the patterns in the sky, pretending they were sea and sand on a beach.

I was one of the lucky ones. We had space to play indoors and outdoors and we were left to our own devices for much of the day during school holiday times, expected to amuse ourselves. TV did not start until late afternoon so on rainy days we spent a lot of time reading – not because we were naturally bookworms, but because the stories took us into another world of people and adventure. This 'inner world' of imagination sometimes seemed more real than life going on in the household. We would pretend to be characters in the story, and simple objects created our scenery indoors and outdoors.

Outdoor play involves far more than simply exercise. It arouses and tickles the senses – the sound of running water, the smell of the sea, damp leaves in autumn and pine woods. In addition to simply providing a sense of well-being, these experiences have fed the creative genius of artists, poets, writers and musicians for generations. Examples of composers 'mood painting' with music include Beethoven's 6th Pastoral Symphony, Vaughan Williams' The Lark Ascending and Delius' On Hearing the First Cuckoo in Spring. Studies have shown that time spent amidst nature has a positive influence on health but we do not really need studies to tell us this. Nature is the natural order of things and civilisation, or man's attempt to tame it, actually tends to intercede to create order for society, effectively reducing the direct influence of nature on daily living.

Children are also remarkably resilient, a reminder of the sheer power of 'life's longing for itself'[18] and they will develop not only because of what parents, carers and the environment provide, but also despite them. This is a comforting reminder that it is sufficient to be a 'good enough' parent and that at the extreme end of the scale, 'the best can be the enemy of the good'.[19] However, if as societies we are ever to provide a level playing field for children as they enter formal education, then we should be looking to provide all children with ample opportunity to discover and develop within the physical world, not only in the early years but throughout childhood.

Is your child steady? Are they ready? Now they can go...

[1]   Fisher, R, 1996. Personal communication.

[2]   Hebb, D O, 1949. *The Organization of behavior: A neuropsychological theory*. New York. Wiley and Sons.

[3]   Brown R M, Milner, P M, 2003. 'The legacy of Donald O. Hebb: More than the Hebb Synapse'. Nature Reviews *Neuroscience* 4/12, 1013–1019.

[4]   Brown R E, 2006. The life and work of Donald Olding Hebb. *Acta Neurologica Taiwanica*, 15/5:127–142.

[5]   National Literacy Trust 2005. 'Why do many young children lack basic language skills?' A discussion paper prepared by the National Literacy Trust's Talk To Your Baby campaign. February 2005. http://www.literacytrust.org.uk/assets/0000/1151/discussionpaper.pdf

[6]   I CAN, 2004. Nursery workers' poll says, 'Turn off the TV'. www.ican.org.uk/news/newsasp?NewsReference=55

[7]   Zeedyk S, The science of human connection. How buggies shape babies' brains. http://suzannezeedyk.co.uk/wp2/2014/04/03/how-buggies-shape-babies-brains/. Accessed 8.8.2016.

[8]   Blaiklock K, 2013. Talking with children when using prams while shopping NZ. *Research in Early Childhood Education Journal*, 16:15–28.

[9]   Lane C, 2010. Self-Voice. A major rethink. Bridgewater. A.R.R.O.W Tuition Ltd.

[10]   Silva K, 2000. Evidence to the House of Commons Select Committee on Education and Employment. First Report.

[11]   Olson H H, Hergenhahn R R, 2013. *An introduction to theories of learning*. Upper Saddle River. NJ Pearson.

[12]   Blythe P, McGlown D J, 1979. *An organic basis for neuroses and educational difficulties*, p.93. Chester. Insight Publications.

[13]   Bejerot S, Plenty S, Humble A, Humble M B, 2013. Poor motor skills: A risk marker for bully victimization. *Aggressive Behaviour*, 39/6:453–461.

[14]   Lebowitz S, 2016. Disturbing science suggests your walk could make you a target for crime. http://uk.businessinsider.com/walk-can-make-you-target-for-crime-2016-7?r=US&IR=T. Accessed 12.10.16.

[15]   Diaz R M, Berk, L E, 1992. *Private speech: From social interaction to self-regulation*. Lawrence Erlbaum.

[16]   Vygotsky L S. 1988. Thinking and speech. In RW Rieber & AS.Carton (Eds.), *The collected works of LS. Vygotsky, Volume 1: Problems of general psychology* (pp. 39–285). New York. Plenum Press. (Original work published 1934.)

[17]   Dixon P, 1988. *Grow your own poems*. Villasavary, France. Pêche Luna Publishers.

[18]   Gibran K, 1996. *The Prophet*. Wordsworths Classics of Literature.

[19]   Fiennes J, 1983. Personal communication.

Chapter 8

Time to Begin

Children in the United Kingdom must receive education from the start of the term following their fifth birthday to the last Friday in June in the school year they turn 16. Most admission authorities in Wales offer places in the reception class of a school in the September after a child's fourth birthday and parents can choose to send their children to pre-school before they turn five, but this is not obligatory.

Whereas in other countries formal instruction in reading and writing does not begin until the ages of six or seven, there is an expectation outlined by the Department of Education in the United Kingdom that children should have acquired a set of basic skills and understanding by the time of school entry.[1] While this document plays lip service to the fact that 'children develop and learn in different ways and at different rates', the framework sets out assessment expectations for children who spend time in early years provision, including children with special educational needs and disabilities.

The Early Years Foundation Stage (2014) expects children to develop competency in seven areas of learning:
- Communication and language
- Physical development
- Personal, social and emotional development
- Literacy

- Mathematics
- Understanding the world
- Expressive arts and design

Some children are enthusiastic and ready to start tackling formal aspects of literacy at four years of age, while others may not be ready for a further two to three years. Rudolf Steiner and Louise Bates Ames both observed that readiness for reading seems to coincide with other signs of biological development such as shedding the first milk teeth, usually starting from around six years of age. Children who are not reading before this age may not necessarily be showing signs of a reading difficulty, but simply demonstrating the natural variations which occur in rates of development for specific skills. Boys can be at a particular disadvantage in this respect if measured against girls of the same age on specific skills.

A statement released in July 2016 by Save the Children said that a quarter of boys in England – 90,000 – started reception class struggling to speak a full sentence or follow instructions.[2] Differences in the *rates* of development at different stages between boys and girls have long been known.

The report, based on a study at the University of Bristol, said that children who start school behind often never catch up.[3] The problem is not with the fundamental gender differences in rates of development (boys do catch up later on), but that the education system fails to recognise these biological differences and accommodate them. The findings also raise questions as to whether modern child-rearing environments in which children have less physical space in which to play than previous generations, and spend more time engaged with e-media, is having a greater effect on boys.

Boys and girls are different. Males, often viewed as the physically stronger sex, are actually more vulnerable in the early years than females, suffering a significantly higher rate of spontaneous abortion, premature birth, infant mortality, a range of illnesses in the early years including ear, nose and throat infections, and a tendency to be fussier and more irritable in infancy. They are also more likely to suffer from developmental disorders including autism, attention deficit disorder and dyslexia.

Greater susceptibility to this range of problems is thought to result from a combination of larger brain size and slower rate of maturation before birth, the presence of only one X chromosome and exposure to higher levels of pre-natal testosterone. Testosterone depresses the functioning of the immune system.

While girls appear to have advantages in the early years, the scales start to balance at puberty, when girls' growth and maturation slows down about two years earlier than that of boys. By the mid-twenties many earlier biological developmental differences in learning outcomes level off, provided that both sexes have enjoyed equal opportunity to develop in ways supportive of gender-specific learning needs. Despite many recognised behavioural differences between the sexes, differences in the architecture of the brain are surprisingly small and are thought to result largely from pre-natal exposure to different hormones, particularly testosterone. The effects of small differences in hormonal environment increase with time and at different stages of development, resulting in divergence in how the brains of boys and girls function.[4]

The most profound difference between girls and boys is in the sequence of development of the various brain regions. A study published in 2007 demonstrated that there is no overlap in the trajectories of brain development in girls and boys, showing that they develop different skills at different times and in different ways. These natural differences are reinforced by nurture, cultural expectations and experience.[5] If genes and hormones set the scene, experience can amplify or diminish differences, raising the question: How can education foster and accommodate these different rates of maturation, needs and learning styles to bring out the best in both boys and girls?

What Are Some of the Acknowledged Differences between Boys and Girls?

(Note that these are general differences and there can be considerable individual variation on specific criteria.)

- Boys grow more quickly than girls from early on in gestation and male cells have a higher metabolic rate, making them potentially more vulnerable to damage at stages of rapid proliferation.

- Boys have a slower rate of maturation in the respiratory and immune systems before birth, making them more susceptible to illnesses in the early years.

- Boys' brains are about nine percent larger than female brains, but girls mature at a physiologically faster rate up to puberty.

- More boys than girls suffer fetal distress during the birth process, and have lower Apgar scores at birth, rendering them more vulnerable to damage.

- Newborn boys secrete more stress hormone in response to a surprising stimulus than girls, making them more reactive to certain stimuli.

- Girls are ahead of boys in the early aspects of expressive language, including use of gesture and first words (about one month earlier), vocabulary growth (about two months earlier in toddler-hood) and about 15 percent more verbally fluent than boys at four to five years of age. There is no difference in receptive language at five years of age.

- Boys are generally better at visuospatial tasks, while girls are ahead in verbal skills.

- Boys are usually superior in strength and endurance in gross motor skills but slower at developing fine motor skills.

- Boys are physically more active and impulsive, and less likely to calm themselves than girls.[6]

What Are the Positive Aspects of Male Differences and How Can These Be Nurtured in the Educational Environment?

The male brain is wired to respond in external, rather than internal, ways. This can leave boys at a disadvantage in a school environment, when teaching focuses on the sedentary development of verbal skills at the expense of active learning. As early as kindergarten, kinetic, impulsive boys are told to sit down, be quiet, and do their work. Teachers are expected to provide a calm, controlled classroom, but boys tend to learn by doing, and if activity in the classroom is suppressed they need to 'let off steam' in other physical ways.

Regular physical activity can be introduced easily into the school day. The

'Fit for Learning' programme is one example. Developed by Professor Pat Preedy and Chris Lees at a primary school in the Midlands, 'Fit for Learning' enables teachers to break up learning sessions with physical activities. The sessions are led by teachers and require no preparation, minimum space and resources. In its early days, staff reported significant improvements in children's coordination, behaviour and concentration. These empirical findings mirror standard practice in other cultures such as Japan and Taiwan, where twice as many recesses are incorporated into the school day in the early years while educational attainment remains high.

Normal attention span is approximately equivalent to three to five minutes per year of a child's age. Therefore, a two-year-old should be able to concentrate on a particular task for up to six minutes, and a child entering kindergarten should be able to concentrate for 15 minutes. The longer a child has to sit still beyond his or her natural attention span, the greater the amount of fidgeting, vocal activity and general disruption. In Finland, pre-school education pays particular attention to the physical needs of children, incorporating up to two hours of outdoor play into the preschool day, enabling boys to work off their physical energy while encouraging girls to develop gross motor skills, resulting in a more level playing field when all children begin formal instruction in reading at seven years of age.

Boys need extra encouragement to develop verbal skills in the early years, because reading ability grows out of spoken language. Language develops through use, not just through passive listening. 'Sounding out' is an important precursor to being able to decode visual symbols phonologically, and sounding out begins with speech, conversation, telling stories and singing. Singing, sometimes erroneously regarded as a 'girl' activity, can help prepare the voice, the eye and the brain for reading, and is suited to boys because it involves active learning. Aforementioned examples of cathedral choristers show how regular singing can enhance every aspect of academic learning.

Physical readiness also plays an important part in a child's ability to sit still, pay attention, hold and control a writing implement and to transfer thoughts via the motor system on to paper. While boys' gross motor skills are generally more robust than those of girls, they tend to struggle for longer to master fine motor skills. Problems with writing can be minimised by separating the mechanics of writing from cognitive processing, teaching penmanship as one skill and encouraging them to talk about ideas and answers before putting them on to paper.

Rough and tumble play is also important for boys because it allows children to explore in creative ways and to test boundaries of strength and control without aggression. In ancient Greece, athletics and wrestling were important elements of a boy's education, as control of the body was considered essential training for the mind. Wrestling was used to develop control of strength and of temper. All healthy young mammals engage in rough and tumble play, and there is a correlation between the appearance of this type of activity and maturity in the frontal lobes of the brain, which are involved in creativity, imagination, empathy, planning and self-control.

One reason suggested by leading scientist Jaak Panksepp for the increasing incidence of ADHD amongst children (particularly boys) may be:

> … the diminishing availability of opportunities for pre-school children to engage in natural self-generated social play. Pre-clinical work indicates that play can facilitate behavioural inhibition in growing animals, while psychostimulants (ritalin for example) reduce playfulness. The idea that intensive social play interventions, throughout early childhood, may alleviate ADHD symptoms remains to be evaluated. As an alternative to the use of play-reducing psychostimulants, society could establish play "sanctuaries" for at-risk children in order to facilitate frontal lobe maturation and the healthy development of pro-social minds.[7]

These recommendations were confirmed by Dr Abigail Norfleet James, author of *Teaching the Male Brain*.[8] She said that boys and girls have distinct skills, with boys generally being less verbal, having less acute hearing, slower perceptual speed and being less likely to be able to control their impulses. While boys generally have better spatial skills and more acute vision, they learn best through touch, are more impulsive, more physically active and are 'movement orientated' throughout primary and secondary education.[9]

If boys and girls are to have equality of opportunity in education, then education needs to take these small but significant differences in rates of maturation and learning needs into account from the outset.

In Finland early education takes a different approach. Children do not start formal instruction in reading until seven years of age and compulsory education finishes at fifteen, but despite this relatively short time spent in statutory education, Finland now boasts the best readers in the world.[10] The Finnish system recognises that before the age of seven, children learn best when they are playing and are then keen to learn by the time they start school. Initially reading lags behind peers in other countries, but catches up and soon overtakes them.

Pre-school, a relatively new phenomenon in Finland, is from six years of age and is optional, but most choose to attend. Preschool is non-academic, and no clear academic targets are set, with socialisation into school culture and learning to work together with other children being the guiding principle. After every 45-minute lesson, children have recess for 15 minutes (giving them time to move and play).

The entire ethos surrounding education is different. Teaching is a highly esteemed and competitive profession, with a 40:1 ratio of applicants for job places and all teachers must have a minimum of a master's degree. Teachers must take a free three-year graduate school preparation programme and they spend nearly half of their time in high-level professional development, collaborative planning, and working with parents.

While some of the success of the system in Finland is attributed in large part to their demographics, high standard of living, largely homogeneous population, a strong national culture, and a completely transparent alphabet code, an education system which works alongside principles of child development is a contributory factor.

In contrast, the statutory framework for early years education in the United Kingdom expects that at the completion of the Early Years Foundation Stage children should have reached set standards in the basics of reading, writing and maths. The framework (2014) lists the following:

A child should be able to:

Read and understand simple sentences. They use phonic knowledge to decode regular words and read them aloud accurately. The also read some common irregular words. They demonstrate understanding when talking to others about what they have read.

Use their phonic knowledge to write words in ways which match their spoken sounds. They also write some irregular common words. They write simple sentences which can be read by themselves and others. Some words are spelt correctly and others phonetically plausible.

Children count reliably with numbers from one to 20, place them in order and say which number is one more or one less than a given number. Using quantities and objects, they add and subtract two single-digit numbers and count on or back to find the answer. They solve problems, including doubling, halving and sharing.[11]

As set out above, the system expects children to be using written symbols by the age of five. Such early expectations tend to force providers of early years care into channelling their instruction through formal teaching methods and practice of specific skills.

Contrast this with an example from pre-school education at a Steiner school in the south of England I visited some years ago. As we sat on a small stone wall drinking coffee at break time, the teacher remarked that the children had built the wall. As the wall comprised large blocks of stone, I could not believe that three, four and five year olds could have done this.

'Oh, they have help in physically moving and placing the blocks', the teacher said, 'but everything else they do under teacher guidance. First they have to look at the space where the wall will be built and sort through a pile of blocks to decide how they will be put together. They wear waterproof clothing and boots and they mix the cement. With adult help, they place the blocks. At the end of each session we count how many they have used and how many are left. By the time the wall is built they understand the rudiments of measurement, weight, counting and subtraction and have just learned the first lesson in quantity surveying! When they start to learn about these things in school, they already understand the concept of numbers, addition, subtraction, space, weight etc. They have also had great fun in the process.'

Recognising that families have to fit within the education system that is currently in place, how can they help their children to be ready for the demands of the curriculum?

Understanding child development is the key; not in an academic sense – there are many books, checklists and professionals available to carry out developmental checks – but in the practical sense of providing a balance of environmental opportunity, experience, engagement, emotional security, discipline (in the true sense of the word, meaning 'to teach') and helping children to build on success. As children develop they try to adapt to their environment, beginning with obvious physical developments in mastery of the body in space but also in linking sensory information to memory. Memories are stored in the brain cells, and without memory, 'we are unable to recognise later what we have seen and heard, and we cannot categorise and understand it either'.[12] Activity and experience are crucial to this process of integrating physical experience with understanding. This process was eloquently described by Jonny Kiphard – known at one time as the 'Grandfather of Motorology' in Germany – a professor who would still dress up as a clown when working with children.

> In the course of its development the child learns to make better and better use of its mind and body. It constantly wants to learn new things using all its senses and muscles. Each child has, of course, its own individual capacity to learn. But it is absolutely decisive which opportunities to learn the parents provide even for the infant.
>
> By opportunities is not, however, meant the stubborn or constant hammering in of knowledge. This method successively suppresses the child's natural ability to learn and its joy at making progress. With mentally retarded children one cannot do without a certain learning programme so that they can cope, at least to some extent, with their life. On the other hand, ambitious parents can ruin the healthy child's desire to learn if they apply force and pressure.

Rather, learning should be an adventurous and successful game. An ancient law for learning says that success in learning is greatest in a happy and relaxed atmosphere.

The child's environment is his natural teacher. Every hill, every tree demands to be climbed. Every wall is there to be balanced on, every ditch to be jumped over. Every bar tempts to gymnastics and every vehicle is there to be pushed, pulled or driven.[12]

He goes on to say that basically parents simply need to offer their children the right thing at the right time – easier said than done – unless parents are observant of what their child can already do and sympathetic towards what they cannot. This is not the same as 'helicopter parenting', the name given to intensive parenting in which mothers tend to hover over their children all the time or 'tiger mothers' who push their children to become high achievers. Studies have found that mothers in particular who practise this type of parenting are more likely to be unhappy, and benefits to children are inconclusive.[13] Effective and 'good enough' parenting helps to support children in learning when they need it, and does not force them to attempt activities which are in advance of their developmental capabilities. The key to learning success is to meet the child where he or she is in terms of their development.

Parenting is one of the hardest jobs we ever do. In an age where we have come to expect maximum working hours, minimum pay and adequate training in the work place, we take on the role of parenting for life without an instruction manual, holidays or pay. Seen in this context the instinct to parent is much stronger than is generally appreciated and is truly an act of love, but that instinct is also informed and nurtured by the type of parenting and family life parents themselves received as children. Increasingly, new generations are embarking on parenthood without having experienced full-time parenting as children. While nursery and early years education can provide an enriched and structured environment for young children, this style of early childhood is a very different experience to growing up in less-advanced societies in which children witness first hand birth and death, breastfeeding and co-sleeping, hunting, foraging, sowing, harvesting, care of younger siblings and the intergenerational dealings of daily life. Much more time is spent in these societies in social interaction and activities unique to the culture.

Children learn by example and modelling the behaviour of those around them. In contrast children in full-time nursery care do not learn the art and skills of parenting through example. It must be learned later 'on the job', and many set out as parents with scant knowledge of the processes of development.

Developmental checklists, once the guarded preserve of the health professional, are now freely available on-line.[14] While parents should not get overly concerned about how their child compares to these checklists, they can be useful if you suspect that your child is not developing either generally or in a specific area of functioning, and as *guidelines* as to what to expect. It is important to remember that guidelines are general and there can be considerable individual variation within these parameters.

Motor development, vision, hearing and language are particularly important in the first three years of life, and any concerns about these should be mentioned to your health visitor or GP, who are the primary source of contact for parents concerned about aspects of their child's development. Referral may then be made to a specialist or other health professional for assessment and possible intervention.

Problems related to hearing, vision or motor skills do not necessarily manifest themselves as obvious defects in these areas, sometimes showing up as behavioural problems. Behavioural signs associated with congestion of the ear, nose or throat and/or primary hearing deficit can include a *combination* of the following:

Hearing:
- Poor sleeping
- Snoring
- Mouth breathing
- Nasal congestion
- Dribbling
- Delayed speech

- Unclear speech
- Need for frequent repetition
- Mishearing or misinterpretation of speech sounds
- Inability to pronounce certain sounds
- Does not respond when spoken to
- Does not respond when spoken to out of eyesight
- Needs to imitate behaviour/instructions
- Fussy eater
- Continued bedwetting above the age of five
- Inability to follow sequential instructions
- Flat or monotone voice
- Has the TV on very loud
- Short attention span
- Easily distracted, particularly when background noise is present
- Oversensitive to certain sounds
- Easily upset / low tolerance for frustration
- Avoids/dislikes certain environments
- Anxiety

In school aged children:
- Letter confusion when reading, writing and spelling (in school age children)
- Poor reading aloud
- Poor reading comprehension
- Poor spelling

Equally, a child who is hypersensitive to sound may be reluctant to participate in certain activities and gatherings and avoid specific places.

Vision
Symptoms of visual problems will vary according to the type and severity of the defect. Problems with near-distance vision (long sight) can affect attention to, and coordination at, near-distance activities including fine motor coordination, reading and writing; conversely, problems with far-distance vision (short sight) will affect far-distance activities. In his book, *The World Through Blunted Sight,*

Patrick Trevor-Roper examined the ways in which defective vision affects far more than eyesight, potentially influencing character, creativity and style, and choice of activities.[15]

> In describing the myopic (short-sighted) personality, different traits are explained in the context of vision. For example, it was said of the myopic child that:
>
>> He cannot do well in the playground because he cannot see. He will not like to hunt because he cannot see the game or the sights of his gun. He will not like to tramp because distance objects are poorly seen, and for that reason, not appreciated... but in school the situation is different, it is so easy to see and so wonderful to read... the child who knows that he cannot excel over his fellows in games gets a big satisfaction out of the conquest of the mind that he can command... he sees the fine details. He does not count in athletics or parties, he is not one-of-the bunch.[16]
>
> On the other hand, of the long sighted child:
>
>> His teachers have said of him that he is lazy, a mischief-maker, dumb, inattentive, or more sympathetic teachers have said that he is 'motor-minded'. His parents insist that he is bright enough but won't study... The motor-minded boy does not correct his classmates when they make a slight mistake and so they like him. He cares nothing for fine details, indeed he does not know that they exist... He is one of the boys; hail fellow, well met, and a jolly good fellow, and why not, he is happy and comfortable, at least when he is not required to do close-work indoors.[17]

In other words, focal range, clarity and coherence can have a strong influence on the activities at which an individual can excel, including attention to detail. Trevor-Roper goes on to suggest that many of the great writers, poets and composers of the past were myopic, forced to concentrate on near-distance activities, and that changes in the style of artists over time can, in many cases, be attributed to deteriorating eyesight. Athletes and sportsmen, on the other hand, may have a tendency to long sight enabling them to see the bigger picture and aim far.

A crossed or wandering eye, which affects three to five percent of children, can result in discrepant focusing between the two eyes, with one eye being more farsighted than the other. If this condition goes untreated, the stronger eye becomes the dominant one and the brain learns to ignore images coming from the weaker eye and stops developing nerve connections leading to it. By the age of nine or ten, the loss of vision in the weaker eye is usually permanent. This type of compromised vision in the weaker eye is termed amblyopia or lazy eye, and can be treated if detected early on.

These are only a few examples of visual problems which over time affect far more than just vision, if not corrected early. As mentioned in the example of amblyopia above, brain centres involved in the perception of visual stimuli are susceptible to wasting if they do not receive clear or coherent sensory information in the first years of life. Any concerns about your child's eyesight should be discussed with the family doctor or optometrist.

Symptoms of possible visual problems:
- Squinting or tilting the head to see better
- Frequent eye rubbing
- Sensitivity to light and/or excessive tearing
- Closing one eye to read, watch TV or see better
- Holding objects very close
- Motion sickness
- Complaining of headaches or tired eyes
- Dropping things; consistently clumsy
- Anxiety

In school-aged children:
- Complains of blurred vision
- Consistently sitting too close to the TV or holding a book too close
- Avoiding activities which require near vision, such as reading or homework, or distance vision, such as participating in sports or other recreational activities
- Losing his place while reading or using a finger to guide his eyes when reading

- Problems with depth perception, heights and figure ground
- Intermittent double vision
- Reading fatigue and headaches after reading for a short time
- Poor reading comprehension
- Frequently loses place when reading
- Short attention span

Motor skills

Motor skills and postural stability both support the functioning of centres involved in the control of eye movements, necessary for reading, writing, copying, catching a ball etc. and reflect integration in the functioning of related systems. If your child does show signs of delay in motor skills, your GP might initially refer him/her to a paediatrician who may then refer on for further assessments and possible treatment to be carried out by a physiotherapist or occupational therapist. While the health system will pick up pathology and those children exhibiting definite delay in achieving motor milestones and related motor skills, it does not have the resources to provide treatment for children who have minor delays in aspects of motor development. These are the children who tend to slip through the system – not quite bad enough to warrant medical attention, nor quite good enough to meet the demands of the classroom.

Neuromotor immaturity is not always symptom specific, and like problems with vision or hearing can manifest itself through behaviour. Behaviour is a form of language. If a child does not have the inner resources it needs to meet the demands of its environment, he or she will regress in how they act and react. Behaviour of this nature may be paradoxical in the sense that superficially it appears to be inappropriate to the situation, but in reality it may be fulfilling a function. Examples of this type of behaviour include children with hyper-sensitive hearing who hum, rock or carry out other self-stimulatory behaviours in noisy environments to shut out unwanted or painful external sounds; children who seem to ignore instructions or commands, not out of rudeness or defiance but because they are slower at processing auditory information; or children who have hypo-sensitive vestibular functioning, who tend to spin, swing or rock excessively trying to increase input to the vestibular system. Others will use avoidance tactics, apparently refusing to take part in activities or go to places in which they feel overwhelmed by sensory stimuli or are aware that they cannot fit in with the crowd or succeed.

Tantrums, often simply the result of thwarted will, can also be an indication of a child who is easily overloaded and who has a low tolerance threshold for frustration. Even adults, when stressed, will regress in how they behave, becoming more short tempered and physically reactive. As emotional arousal increases, the ability to express feelings and needs through rational language (a higher brain function) tends to decrease. The shorter the fuse, the faster it will ignite, and children who lack basic skills tend to become stressed and frustrated more easily.

This group of 'grey area' children will often benefit from general play programmes or non-invasive therapies to help provide them with the tools not only for formal learning but also for life in general. Various programmes are available to help parents provide general activities in the context of play.

One such programme developed in Australia and now available in several European countries is 'Gymbaroo', which focuses on putting the 'natural' back into development:

> In our natural evolutionary past, nature provided much of the necessary stimuli, and we evolved to imbed these into our natural developmental processes. A simple analogy: it is accepted as basic knowledge that play in baby animals is about developing later survival skills for when they are adults. So is it reasonable to take the 'natural' out of life and still expect our children to maximise their future learning abilities? GymbaROO was founded in 1982 on the premise that the neurological development of the young child is integrally linked to later learning and development.[18]

The programme provides an effective and comprehensive series of classes for babies and parents from six weeks to school-aged children. The classes are based on the appropriate sensory and movement experiences required for healthy brain development. It stresses that it does not focus on making children better than everyone else but aims to help children develop to their own potential, whatever that may be. It is play based and is a fun activity for parents and children to do together on a regular basis, also providing an often much-needed social forum for parents.

Speech

Recognising speech and language delay in pre-school children is important because the ability to use written language is based upon the foundation of spoken language. Parents need information about the range of normal development, so they can spot early problems and seek help if appropriate.

> Speech and language delays affect six to seven per cent of children at school entry and can result in problems in one or more areas, such as understanding vocabulary and grammar, inferring meaning, expressive language, sound production, voice, fluency and articulation, and the use of language in social contexts. For some children, language problems are markers for – and secondary to – conditions such as autism, sensory impairment, or more general developmental disabilities. For others, they are the result of primary delay that cannot be accounted for by low non-verbal ability, hearing impairment, behaviour problems, emotional problems, or neurological impairments. Environmental factors such as limited opportunities for learning language or learning English as an additional language may also overlap with primary and secondary delay. Language delay that persists until school entry can have adverse effects on literacy, behaviour, social development, and mental health into adulthood, with receptive language and secondary delay particular risk factors.[19]

Standard assessment of children with speech and language delay should include thorough investigations for hearing impairment, functioning of the vocal and oral tracts and motor aspects of speech. If no abnormality in these areas is detected, speech therapy, particularly in the first three years can make a significant difference.

If there has been a history of frequent ear, nose or throat infections in the first three years of life, although children tend to grow out of these with time, hearing can be impaired for several weeks after the acute phase of infection has cleared up. If a child has suffered two or three infections a year in the first three years, hearing may have been affected for several months at the critical stage for 'tuning in' to the sounds specific to the mother tongue. Although hearing recovers, this temporary period of impaired hearing can result in later difficulty discriminating between similar sounds such as *s* and *f, f* and *th, sh* and *ch, p* and *b, m* and *n, w* and *r,* etc. As the pathways involved in processing auditory stimuli are entrained primarily in the pre-school years, a history of intermittent hearing impairment in the early years can continue to affect the brain's interpretation of auditory stimuli later on. This type of difficulty, which is specific to the neurological pathways involved in perceiving auditory stimuli (as opposed to hearing or primary language impairment), can sometimes be helped with the use of specific sound therapy programmes later on.

Does Routine Screening Children for Developmental Delays Prevent Learning Problems?

General knowledge of the processes involved in normal child development can help parents and professionals to recognise when a child needs professional assessment and to receive extra help or support. However, a study published in 2016 suggests that *routine* screening of very young children for developmental delays, who seem fine to their parents and paediatrician, does not reduce the chances that they will have learning difficulties and other problems later.[20] In an article based on the findings of this study Sharon Begley reported how:

> This is not about parents and paediatricians watching for signs of delays in speech, language, motor, and other skills by observing one- to four-year-olds in ordinary interactions or at doctor visits. That, especially doctors' expert judgement, is worthwhile, experts agree. The question is, instead, about the value of standardized questionnaires that are filled out by parents and meant to uncover unnoticed developmental delays. Logically, it seems such screening should be beneficial. Why not uncover overlooked cases? And how can intensive interventions not help put little kids flagged by such screening on course for normal development? Surprisingly, scientific support for both propositions is shaky.[21]

The article goes on to say:

> The flimsiness of research on the benefits of screening is a longstanding
> problem. In 2015 the US Preventive Services Task Force, a panel of outside
> physicians and other experts who make health care recommendations to the
> government, reported that there is no evidence to answer the overarching
> question of whether screening for speech and language delay or disorders
> improves speech and language outcomes.[22] It found insufficient evidence to
> recommend for or against general screening with there being a danger that
> over-anxious parents using general screening questionnaires identify their
> normally developing child as having a problem, which when examined by
> a developmental expert or paediatrician is found not to be the case.[21]

In other words, routine screening was throwing up 'false positives', causing
unnecessary anxiety to parents and clogging up the system. The screening
tools also failed to catch many children who were developmentally delayed.

Some experts argue that it does not help a child to be identified as
developmentally delayed unless he or she then receives interventions that
obviate or diminish learning difficulties and other common consequences
of developmental delays. This is certainly true, but there is also a case to be
made for formal recognition that a problem exists (diagnosis) so that effective
strategies and support can be put in place in the longer-term future.

Others argue in favour of routine screening for developmental delays. In
the USA the American Academy of Paediatrics recommends that children
undergo developmental screening – checklists and questionnaires – at ages
18 months and 30 months, in addition to paediatricians observing them for
delays at nearly every visit. In the United Kingdom children are not seen by
a paediatrician as a matter of routine unless a problem is suspected, and are
therefore more likely to slip through the net. Those who argue in favour of
routine screening point out that absence of evidence to support the benefits
of screening is not evidence of absence of need, but rather a lack of studies to
support the belief that early intervention can make a difference.

Failure to acknowledge that an underlying problem exists makes it easy for
children to be mislabelled as 'lazy', 'could to better', oppositional or 'doing as

well as can be expected'. The latter is a trap teachers fall into if a child seems to be performing well enough. Bright children with neuromotor immaturity (NMI) can often compensate for their underlying difficulties to some degree, reaching minimum required standards in class but at the expense of under-achieving.

Pilot studies carried out in schools in the Midlands and London[*] have provided empirical evidence to support the relationship between immature neuromotor skills and educational performance. Both studies carried out simple tests for neuromotor maturity in primary school children.[23] They then compared the results on the physical tests to national curriculum measures of achievement. The schools in the Midlands found that in a sample of 262 children aged six to seven years, children with the least mature neuromotor skills were performing in the lowest quartiles on national curriculum tests and vice-versa.[24] The school in London found that 100 percent of pupils who scored below age-related expectations at the end of Year Two in reading, showed high (above 30 percent) percentages of neuromotor immaturity. The lower the national curriculum (NC) level (i.e. level one), the higher the average neuromotor immaturity percentage score. Pupils with the highest neuromotor immaturity (between 65 percent and 78 percent) scored the lowest (NC level one) in reading, writing and maths.[25]

Can Anything Be Done Later On?

The INPP clinical programme (see Chapters Three and Five) was designed to be used with children from seven years of age and upwards when clear signs of neuromotor immaturity are present. The reasons for waiting until seven years of age before intervening with this individualised programme are threefold:

1. The nervous system undergoes a major period of myelination and neural pruning between six and a half and eight years of age, meaning that a child can appear to be uncoordinated and struggling with aspects of formal learning at six years of age, only for many of these difficulties to recede naturally by the age of eight.

2. Due, in part, to the above and dynamic changes which take place in the

[*] Grove School Birmingham, Woodlands Academy Walsall, and John Stainer Community School, Brockley, London.

course of normal development, children under the age of seven are slower to respond to the INPP clinical programme. If starting at six, the programme can take 18 months to achieve its aims and may need a 'top up' a year later; if started after seven, the average duration of the programme is 12 months.

3. The INPP clinical exercises need to be carried out slowly and precisely. Children under the age of seven can find this difficult to do.

Children under the age of seven respond best to less structured, play-based movement programmes, unless the presenting problems are so severe they warrant intensive specialist therapy.

Evidence collected at INPP over many years indicates that the observations of child development experts in the past (Gesell, Ames, Steiner, Montessori) are still correct – that although some children are ready to tackle formal aspects of learning from an earlier age, it is not abnormal for some children not to be ready to read and write fluently before the age of seven.

Problems occur when an educational system insists that 'one size fits all', placing children who are later at developing skills specific to reading, writing and maths at a disadvantage within an increasingly rigid education system which tests children against national averages from an early age. Just as success tends to breed success, repeated failure or under-achievement foster disillusionment, demotivation, lack of self-confidence and stress, all of which are counter-productive to learning. Children who are born in the late spring and summer months are also at a disadvantage as they are biologically some nine to twelve months younger than their peers from the time of school entry throughout their school career. While the gap in biological differences tends to close with time, the potential gaps in achievement resulting from being placed within a set of group expectations before a child is developmentally ready tend to grow with time, and can have a lasting impact on achievement, confidence and aspiration. Education should not be a lottery partly based on the accident of birth date. If it is ever to provide a truly level playing field, children's biological age, as opposed to chronological age set against a national intake date, should play an equal part in determining when a child must start school.

Gymbaroo has the right approach in aiming to help parents in the pre-school years understand how nature provides the ingredients children need to thrive. The stories and songs outlined in previous chapters of this book, available on the accompanying CD, give parents a 'starter pack' of ideas and developmentally appropriate activities they can play with their children from three years of age and upwards.

Humankind as we know it today is the product of some eight million years of evolution, in which brain and body together underwent adaptations, and which have culminated in the 'modern' mind. The development of every child follows a similar principle adapted to the changing demands of societies over time through the process of enculturation. While there are general milestones which children are expected to reach within certain time frames, 'faster' and 'higher' are not necessarily better. Lifestyles and social and educational expectations change with each generation and vary across cultures, but the developmental needs of children (in common with other mammals) remain relatively constant and are rooted and reflected in the foundations of physical development.

Are your children able to sit comfortably ? Now they are ready to begin...

[1] Department of Education 2014. Statutory framework for learning, development and care for children from birth to five.

[2] Save the Children. The lost boys. How boys are falling behind in their early years. July 2016. http://www.savethechildren.org.uk/resources/online-library/lost-boys.

[3] Moss G, Washbrook L, 2016. Understanding the gender gap in literacy and language development. University of Bristol. Graduate School of Education. http://www.bristol.ac.uk/media-library/sites/education/documents/bristol-working-papers-ineducation/Understanding%20the%20Gender%20Gap%20working%20paper.pdf.

[4] Durden-Smith J, de Simone D, 1983. *Sex and the brain*. London. Pan Books Ltd.

[5] The NIH/NIMH study. 2007. Sexual dimorphism of brain developmental trajectories during childhood and adolescence. *NeuroImage*, 36/4:165–173.

[6] Eliot L, 2009, Pink brain, blue brain. How small differences grow into troublesome gaps – and what we can do about it. New York. Houghton Mifflin Harcourt.

[7] Panksepp J, 2007. Can play diminish ADHD and facilitate the construction of the social brain? *J Can Acad Child Adolesc Psychiatry*, 16/2:57–66.

[8] Norfleet James A, 2007. *Teaching the male brain*. CA. Corwin Press.

[9] Norfleet James A. Presentation at the International Boys' Schools Coalition (IBSC) Conference. London, 19 January 2010.

[10] PISA.

[11] Statutory framework for the Early Years Foundation Stage. Setting the standards for learning, development and care for children from birth to five, 2014. Department for Education, UK.

[12] Kiphard E J, 1990. *Steps of development. A guide to check a child's development.* Broadstairs. Borgman Publishing Ltd.

[13] Rizzo K M, Schiffrin H H and Liss M, 2012. Insight into the parenthood paradox: Mental health outcomes of intensive mothering. *Journal of Child and Family Studies,* DOI: 10.1007/s10826-012-9615-z.

[14] http://www.nhs.uk/Tools/Pages/birthtofive.aspx.

[15] Trevor-Roper P, 1988. *The world through blunted sight.* London. Penguin Books.

[16] Rice T, 1930. Physical defects in character, II, near-sightedness. *Hygea*, 8:644.

[17] Rice, T, 1930. Physical defects in character, I, far-sightedness. *Hygea*, 8:536

[18] http://www.gymbaroo.com.au/contents/philosophy. Accessed 20.09.16.

[19] Boyle J, 2011. Speech and language delays in preschool children. *BMJ* 2011;343:d5181. doi: http://dx.doi.org/10.1136/bmj.d5181 (Published 25 August 2011).

[20] Recommendations on screening for developmental delay (2016). Canadian Task Force on Preventive Health Care. CMAJ Podcasts: author interview at https://soundcloud.com/cmajpodcasts/151437-guide.

[21] Begley S, 2016. Does screening children for developmental delays prevent learning problems? STAT. 04.04.2016. https://www.statnews.com/2016/04/04/developmental-delays-children/?trendmd-shared=1.

[22] Wallace F I et al., 2015. Screening for speech and language delay in children 5 years old and younger: A systematic review. *Pediatrics,* 136/2:e474–e481.

[23] Goddard Blythe S A, 2012. *Assessing neuromotor readiness for learning. The INPP developmental screening test and school intervention programme.* Chichester. Wiley-Blackwell.

[24] Basnett J, Dowell C, Corbett L, Pitt S, 2015. Screening and intervention in schools using the INPP screening test and developmental movement programme. Relationship between neuromotor skills and learning outcomes using national curriculum results and Ofsted expectations. Presented at the Child Development in Education Conference, London, October 2015.

[25] Harte S, 2015. Physical development and National Curriculum levels – the incidence of neuromotor immaturity (NMI) in London primary schools and the relationship between NMI and National Curriculum measures of achievement. Presented at the Child Development in Education Conference, London, October 2015.

Index

A

abstract thinking, 126

accelerationism, 2

action schemas, 125

ADHD, 156

adolescent years, 4

affectionate touch, 26, 28
  lack of, 27

amblyopia, 164

American Academy of Paediatrics, 169

Ames, Louise Bates, 152, 171

Amphibian reflexes, 42

'Are you sitting comfortably?', 1

artists, 145

Ascidian sea squirt, 17

Asperger's syndrome, 5

Asymmetrical Tonic Neck Reflex
  (ATNR), 21–3

ATNR: *see* Asymmetrical Tonic Neck
  Reflex

audio-vocal feedback loop, 52

Auditory Integrative Training, 38

automated function, 7

Ayres, A, Jean, 17

B

babbling, 33

babies
  hearing of, 45
  musical language of, 11
  premature, 35

Babkin reflex, 31–2

balance, 138–9
  beginning of, 138
  control of, 138
  sense of, 74

Banting, Roger, 144

bed wetting:
  Pulgar Marx reflex and, 39

Begley, Sharon, 168

behaviour as language, 165

Berthoz, A, 17

biological needs, 6

bipedalism, 38

birth
  breathing at, 19
  canal, design of, 38
  date, 171

Blaiklock, Dr Ken, 135

blinking reflex, 43

Blythe, Peter, 138

body map, 7

boredom, 141

bottom shuffle, 25

boys, 152
  differences from girls, 152–4
  fine motor skills of, 156
  gross motor skills of, 155–6
  male brain, 154
  brain
  development, 2–3, 166
  frontal lobes of, 156
  hemispheres, 143
  male, 154
  see also neural development,
  neuromotor immaturity, neuronal
  potential, neuroscience

breathing
  at birth, 19

Broca, 33

buggies: forward-facing, 134–5

Butler Hall, B, 38

C

cathedral choirs, 51–2

About the Authors

Sally Goddard Blythe MSc. (Psych.) is Director of the Institute for Neuro-Physiological Psychology (INPP) in Chester. INPP is a private research, practice and training centre in the assessment and remediation of neuromotor immaturity based on the INPP method.

The INPP method was developed by the late Peter Blythe (PhD). Based on standard tests developed and used in mainstream medicine, it comprises a specific method of assessment for signs of neuromotor immaturity in children and adults and a unique remedial programme using exercises which replicate earlier stages of child development to strengthen the neural pathways involved.

Sally has worked in the field of child development for 30 years. She has written extensively on the relationship between physical development, learning achievement and emotional functioning.

She has lectured throughout Europe and parts of the USA providing training in the INPP method to other professional groups and information to parents. She still sees the mainstay of her professional life as working in clinical practice with children and families.

She was married to the late Peter Blythe, has three adult children and seven grandchildren.

Michael Lazarev is a professor of medicine and a musician who has combined the two disciplines to produce musical programmes designed to support the development of the child from pre-conception to seven years of age.

He is head of the Children's Rehabilitatory Medicine Centre in Moscow and the author of *SONATAL* (sound and birth). His book *Mamalayish* containing a vast collection of his songs for parents to use with their children was published in 2010.

Haydn Giffney is narrator of the stories and poems on the 2 CDs. In a career spanning nearly 50 years Haydn has covered nearly all aspects of the entertainment business. He studied drama in Sydney before working as a professional actor both in Australia and in the UK. Until recently he had run his own Youth Theatre School for over 15 years. In addition to his time in theatre he has also worked as a stand-up comic, vocalist and magician.

Although never making the big time as a TV actor, Haydn has had many walk on parts in TV series such as *Howards Way*, *Bergerac* and *Gentlemen and Players*. He now spends most of his time as a professional artist.

Other books from Hawthorn Press

Too Much, Too Soon?
Early learning and the erosion of childhood
Edited by Richard House

In twenty-three hard-hitting chapters, leading educators, researchers, policy makers and parents advocate alternative ways ahead for slowing childhood, better policy-making and, above all, the 'right learning at the right time' in children's growth — learning when they are developmentally ready.

376pp; 234 × 156mm; 978-1-907359-02-6; pb

Games Children Sing & Play
Singing movement games to play with children ages 3–5
Joan Carr Shimer, Valerie Baadh Garrett

This treasury of both old and new games will help children feel at ease in their bodies and build relationships with others. The magic weaving of rhythms, movement, songs, stories and pictures invites children into worlds of vibrant wonder.

128pp; 200 × 250mm; 978-1-907359-20-0; pb

Free to Learn
Steiner Waldorf early childhood care and education
Lynne Oldfield

The approach of Steiner Waldorf kindergartens and childcare centres is that children's early learning is profound, that childhood matters and that the early years should be enjoyed, not rushed through. Lynne Oldfield, Director of the London Steiner Waldorf Early Childhood Teacher Training Course draws on kindergarten experience from around the world, with stories, helpful insights, lively observations and vivid pictures.

240pp; 216 × 138mm; 978-1-907359-13-2; pb

Reclaim Early Childhood

The Philosophy, Psychology and Practice of Steiner-Waldorf Early Years Education

Sebastian and Tamara Suggate

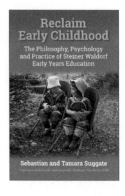

Comparing Steiner-Waldorf pedagogy critically with mainstream early years education, this book presents a lively overview of the philosophical, developmental and educational foundations of Rudolf Steiner-Waldorf early years education. An essential sourcebook for educators, student teachers and academics.

200pp; 234 × 156mm; 978-1-912480-10-4; pb

Writing to Reading the Steiner Waldorf Way

Foundations of Creative Literacy in Classes 1 and 2

Abi Allanson and Nicky Teensma

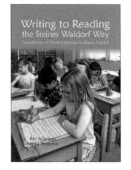

This theory and practice-based book outlines the foundations for creative literacy and teaching children how to write and read. It explores how Steiner/Waldorf pedagogy dovetails with mainstream primary approaches and specialist dyslexia-friendly methods. It offers a holistic, active and creative approach based on the foundation of children's spoken language development.

352pp; 246 × 189 mm; 978-1-907359-88-0; pb

Simplicity Parenting

Using the power of less to raise happy, secure children

Kim John Payne

This is a title for parents who want to slow down, but who don't know how; for families with too much stuff, too many choices and too much information. Here are four simple steps for decluttering, quieting, and soothing family dynamics so that children can thrive at school, get along with peers, and nurture well-being. Using the extraordinary power of less, Kim John Payne, one of the world's leading Steiner-Waldorf educators, offers novel ways to help children feel calmer, happier, and more secure.

352pp; 234 x 156mm; 978-1-912480-03-6; pb

The Parenting Toolkit

Simple Steps to Happy & Confident Children

Caroline Penney

Caroline Penney explains how to help your child become confident, capable, caring, and able to reach their full potential as well as offering advice on how to ensure that you are getting all the self-care that you need in order to be a good parent. Illustrated throughout with warm and witty greyscale by Kate Hajducka.

176pp; 250 × 200mm; 978-1-907359-90-3; pb

Ordering books

If you have difficulties ordering Hawthorn Press books from a bookshop, you can order direct from our website:

www.hawthornpress.com

or the following distributor:

Booksource
50 Cambuslang Road, Glasgow, G32 8NB
Tel: (0845) 370 0063
E-mail: orders@booksource.net

Hawthorn Press

www.hawthornpress.com

CD 1 Wings of Childhood

Words written by Michael Lazarev.

Music written by Michael Lazarev.

Accompanist: Sergei Makaev. Soprano: Donna Fitzpatrick. Bass: James Goddard.

Sound Recordist: Andre Zachesov.

Words translated by Andre Patrekeev.

Director: Michael Lazarev.

Produced at Andre Zachesov sound recording studios, Moscow.

Illustrations: Sharon Lewis.

Copyright: Michael Lazarev.

Sponsored by SONATAL and The Institute for Neuro-Physiological Psychology. (INPP), Chester, UK.

SONATAL: www.sonatal.ru

INPP: www.inpp.org.uk

CD 2 Movement: Your Child's First Language

Story 1: *Early Morning by the Pond*
Written by Sally Goddard Blythe.
Narrated by Haydn Giffney.
Copyright: Sally Goddard Blythe

Story 2: *A Day in the Garden*
Written by Sally Goddard Blythe.
Narrated by Haydn Giffney.
Copyright: Sally Goddard Blythe

Produced by In Ear Entertainment Ltd, Gloucestershire.